Cricket in Australia
1804 – 1884

Bill Hornadge

First Published 2006

Published by

Review Publications Pty. Ltd.
(ABN 19-000 070 655)

P.O. Box 1463, Dubbo 2830, NSW Australia

Other books by Bill Hornadge:

The Australian Slanguage

The Ugly Australian (Quotations)

Lennie Lower – He made a nation laugh

The Hidden History of Australia

The Search for an Australian Paradise

The Journal of John O'Brien

The Poppy Crop (Fiction)

First Printing 2006
ISBN 0-909895-62-7

Published by:

Review Publications Pty Ltd
ABN 19 000 070 655

PO Box 1463, Dubbo 2830
NSW Australia

Bibliographical Notes

- A scrap book of the 1878 Gregory Tour, probably kept by Blackham, containing scores of clippings from the UK regional newspapers, affixed in chronological order of the tour, a gold mine of information on the tour.

- Two giant scrap books of mainly NSW illustrative clippings from 1870's – 1880's yielding lots of illustrative material, alas without dates or origins.

- Archives of Christchurch, New Zealand Public Library.

- Archives of Mitchell Library, Sydney.

- Harper's Magazine, New York, issue of October 19, 1878.

- The Encyclopaedia of Aborigine Australia.

- Cricket Walkabout by D. J. Mulvary, Melbourne University Press.

- The Australian Dictionary of Biography.

- The Australian Encyclopaedia.

- England versus Australia, by David Frith, Collins.

- The A to Z of Australian Cricket, Oxford University Press.

- On Top Down Under – Australian Cricket Captains, by Ray Robinson.

- A History of Cricket, by Trevor Bailey, Cassell.

- Sports, by Keith Dunstan, Cassell.

- Start of Play, by David Underdown, Penguin.

- The Story of Cricket in Australia, by Jack Egan, MacMillian.

- And a personal accumulation of clippings on various aspects of cricket over many decades, far too numerous to detail. Along with many other cricket books read and then passed on to other readers.

Index

Biographical Notes 3

Preface 5

Chapter 1 – In the Beginning 6

Chapter 2 – Rafferty Rules O.K. 10

Chapter 3 – Cricket Down Under 13

Chapter 4 – The Gambling Years 19

Chapter 5 – The First English Tour 22

The Richmond Cricket Ground, Melbourne 1864 26

Chapter 6 – The Second English Tour 27

Chapter 7 – The Aboriginal Tour 28

Dr. W. G. Grace (Portrait) 32

Chapter 8 – The Honeymoon Tour 33

James Lillywhite (Portrait) 40

Chapter 9 – The Lillywhite Tour 41

Chapter 10 – The First Test Matches 46

The Centenary of the First Tests 50

There's Gold in them thar Hills (Trophies) 51

Gentlemen v Professionals 52

Chapter 11 – The Feminine Invasion 54

Dave Gregory (Portrait) 62

Chapter 12 – The Gregory Tour 63

Chapter 13 – Off to a Bad Start 65

Spofforth (Three Cartoons by British Artists) 68

Chapter 14 – The Triumphal Tour 70

Chapter 15 – Tour Summary 78

Chapter 16 – Australia v New York 81

Chapter 17 – The Lord Harris Cometh 85

Chapter 18 – The Birth of the Ashes 90

Cover Design: Adapted from Harper's Bazaar sketch of October 19, 1878
of the Australia versus New York Clubs cricket match.

Preface

There can be no denying that Australia is a nation obsessed with sport of all kinds, with cricket being one of the leaders in this field. No doubt its warm weather throughout most of the year is responsible for its outdoor lifestyle, but there are some puzzling questions that need answers.

How is it that in the later half of the 19th Century, with only a tiny population, did the two main states of New South Wales and Victoria, manage to produce a whole group of cricketers, most of whom were recognised as being leading world players: Spofforth, Bannerman, Blackham, Murdoch, Gregory and Allan, to name a few. All world stars in their categories.

This seems a gigantic task given the fact that in the first sixty years of the century they nurtured the game totally on their own, cut off from the rest of the cricketing world. It was only in the 1860's when English teams started to tour Australia that they made real contact with Britain, the home of cricket.

In this volume I have explored some of these questions and have been able to come up with quite a lot of previously unknown material. Heading this is the chapter solving the mystery of how the English Captain, Lillywhite managed to lose his wicket keeper, Pooley, in Christchurch, New Zealand. I did this by going to Christchurch and digging through the archives of their main Library. A quite interesting story resulted.

And there is a great story of how the women muscled into this new sporting field. And the great Gregory tour of 1878 is dealt with fully, including the team's match against New York, where they nearly came unstuck due to the crafty New Yorkers stacking their team with a former Baseball striker who sent down almost unplayable underarm scrubbers.

On one point I must apologise, and that is that in some cases I cannot supply the exact date or the origin of some illustrative material. This is due to the fact that the material lacked these details when I acquired it many years ago.

Bill Hornadge, Dubbo, 2006

For thousands of years primitive individuals have hit ball like objects with sticks to make up what turns out in the end to be games. One of these games is cricket.

GERMANY A CRICKET NATION!

Well. Surprise. Surprise it actually was right up to the start of World War One when Kaiser Bill put a stop to this bit of British nonsense. The advertising Poster Stamp promoting the Nuremburg Cricket Club shown on the left was issued in 1908. If the Germans had taken up the game again after the war we might have been spared World War II.

A DANISH DELICACY

The Poster Stamp on the left was issued in Denmark in 1913 and was used to promote a brand of margarine. After that Cricket seemed to fade away a bit. Now that the Danes have an Australian Princess perhaps she could get them interested again in the game of Cricket.

CHAPTER 1

In the Beginning

Various games involving sticks and balls have been around in primitive societies for thousands of years, mainly played by the children with adults sometimes joining in. Over time some of these games became formalised with standard rules to become national and even international games.

These games include cricket (the subject of this book), the closely related hockey, baseball, tennis, golf, rounders, polo (for the elite) and polocrosse (in Australia for the plebs). Others have come and after a while, have disappeared. Such as vigaro which had a huge following in Australia schools in the 1920's and 1930's but vanished from the scene during World War II.

Tracing the history and determining the origins of some of these games can be a tricky business due to conflicting claims. For example the French have long claimed that it was they who invented cricket and then exported it across the English Channel after the unpleasantness of 1066. And they have ancient murals to support these claims, much to the dismay and chagrin of the Brits. So we must tread carefully here.

What can't be denied is the fact that even if cricket did not originate in Britain, it was the British who took it up, nurtured it carefully and eventually exported it successfully to almost every corner of the once great British Empire, including Australia.

Cricket in some form was certainly played in Britain in the Middle Ages, with increasing mention of the game in records from the 14th Century although it did not always receive approval of the Rulers of the day. Oliver Cromwell put a ban on the game being played in Ireland, while there were numerous accounts of players being fined in England for daring to stage games on Sunday.

However, by the 18th Century these obstacles had been overcome and the game had become formalised throughout the British Island by publication of a set of rules in 1744.

The Marylebone Cricket Club (MCC) was founded in London in 1787 and for the first time this ancient game had an established voice to promote it and to change the rules from time to time. It was also a move that split the game (at least in England) into two distinct camps – the Gentry (represented by the Players, later named The Gentlemen) and the Common Heard, mostly represented by village players and (later) by the Professionals, a subject I will deal with in a later chapter.

In the 19th Century the game took a great leap forward when it was adopted by all the leading Public (i.e. Private) schools, and by the military when the Duke of Wellington ordered that cricket grounds be established at all barracks and Academies of the nation. The British Army and Navy were also responsible for taking the game to the far flung outposts of the ever expanding Empire including Australia in 1804.

They were also responsible for re-exporting it across the English Channel to European countries and to various other foreign outposts, though, alas not to America where the Yanks stuck grimly to their own chosen version of the stick and ball game named baseball. Cricket was quite popular in Germany until World War 1 put a sudden end to that experiment. However, cricket still has a toehold among a small band of enthusiasts in Denmark and Holland.

In some of the distant places to which the game has been exported the locals have embraced it with such enthusiasm that in time they were able to trounce some of the best teams that Mother England could field, much to the dismay of the Gentlemen who govern the MCC. But cricket enthusiasts around the world still acknowledge England as the 'home' of the hallowed game.

This painting by Francis Hayman made in the first half of the 18th Century shows an early cricket match in progress. Note the curved end of the bat and the quaint moveable iron device acting as the stumps. Wooden stumps were added to cricket much later on, firstly in two sticks, then three sticks, starting at twelve inches in height at first up to the present sizes. Incidentally, the wicket keeper in this match was Hogarth, a good friend of Hayman.

CHAPTER 2

Rafferty Rules. O.K.

When reading about cricket in the early days it is essential to realise that both the conditions and rules were vastly different to those prevailing today.

The first set of rules of the game were produced in 1744, and endorsed by the MCC in 1787, but they were fairly basic and flexible, and were not universally adopted even in their native country.

Over the years they were constantly amended to suit local conditions, both in England and in the distant colonies where the game was played, and rules in the colonies were often quite different to those in Mother England. All of which was the cause of much confusion when teams from England started to venture abroad in the 1860's. The rules were sometimes changed for individual matches and sometimes were so far from being set in concrete that they resembled the rules of the mythical Mr Rafferty.

Perhaps the main changes over the years related to bowling. The original law called for four ball overs and this was observed for most of the 19th Century. But in 1889 the MCC changed the rules to five balls an over, and in 1900 changed them again to six ball overs. Australia changed to six ball overs in 1887 and then changed to eight ball overs in 1918. The MCC followed suit in 1929 and then everyone changed back to six ball overs in 1945.

In the beginning underarm bowling was universal with fast 'grubbers' along the wicket being widely favoured by the fast bowlers. As a result early bats differed greatly from modern ones as they usually had a curl on the end which enabled the batsman to scoop up and dispatch balls coming along the turf.

One favourite variation for the early bowlers was to hoist the ball high in the air so that it would fall on the stumps. If delivered accurately this was an extremely difficult ball to handle and batsmen often stepped back on the stumps trying to handle the descending ball. On the other hand a ball that fell short of the stumps gave a batsman with a good eye the chance to dispatch it to the boundary for a four or even a six.

Round arm bowling was not introduced into Australia until 1853 but by no means universally popular with bowlers and was optional for the rest of the century. It was used in tandem with various forms of overarm delivery and underarm dispatches.

The MCC evidently forgot to erase underarm bowling from its rules book because it was still legal in 1981, as any New Zealander you meet up with will testify at some length and with some warmth. To every Kiwi the First of February 1981 is etched deep in his memory as cricket's blackest day of shame. It was on that day on the hallowed Melbourne Cricket Ground that Australia was playing New Zealand in a one day International match. With one ball to play the Kiwis needed six runs to win. To prevent them doing this the Aussie Captain Greg Chappell instructed his brother Trevor to deliver the last bowl underarm in the form of an unplayable 'grubber'. Which he did. The reverberations of that distinctly un-gentlemanly act almost sparked a Trans Tasman war. Forgiveness on the part of the Kiwis still seems in the distant future.

Another unusual feature of 19th Century cricket was the breaching of the universal rule that each side should field eleven players. Teams were so unevenly matched in those days that a Captain of the stronger side would allow his weaker opponent to field 18 players. And if the opponent was VERY weak he would allow 22 players on the field. This practice was so widespread that it even extended to teams from England, and to Australian teams playing weaker English sides while on tours of the Old Country, though it was never extended to Test matches.

A strong team of eleven players in a game against a weaker team of 18 or 22 men was said to have played Against the Odds, and this was always noted down in the records of touring teams so they could be distinguished from normal games.

The Against the Odds games had some interesting consequences. With 22 players the outfield became very crowded and it was very difficult for batsmen to penetrate the field of such tight cordons. On the other hand, if a ball was skied it was not unusual for five or six fielders to rush to catch it and some very spectacular collisions.

In those days umpires were not properly trained in the rules, nor were they paid any fees. Often they were conscripted for duty out of the crowd of spectators and they frequently allowed their attention to wander from the game. A regular complaint was that they failed to keep tally of the number of balls bowled in an over, resulting in overs of varying length. At one game in a country match in Australia, the irascible English Captain W.G. Grace, got fed up after he had delivered seven balls in what was supposed to be a four ball over. Hurling the ball to the ground and loudly declaring "Over" woke up the numerically challenged Umpire.

In most important matches each side nominated an umpire which led to eternal disputes of alleged favouritism. In many cases a travelling side came with its own umpire to make sure that at least it got half of a fair go in the game. But decisions by umpires with weak eyesight or bias was a constant complaint in the early matches, and is not unknown in modern ones.

There was one other vast difference between conditions in the 19th Century and today, a difference no MCC could govern. This was the state of the grounds and the pitches. These were always earthen and usually not grassed. The standardised concrete pitches with their coir matting of the early 20th Century were far into the future and the old pitches ranged from fair to bloody awful. Most of them could be summed up as a bowler's paradise and a batsman's nightmare, and this was directly responsible for the low scoring matches of the 19th Century when a century score was a bit of a miracle for any batsman to achieve.

Erratic pitches and overgrown outfields (in Australia) and semi swamps (in England), indifferent umpiring of the 19th Century which makes some of their achievements outlined in the pages that follow are very remarkable indeed.

CHAPTER 3

Cricket Down Under

Officially the start of cricket in Australia commences on January 8, 1804, with the first mention of the game in print in the Sydney Gazette as follows:

"The late intense weather has been favorable to the amateurs of cricket, who have scarcely lost a day for the last month. The frequent immoderate heats might have been considered inimical to the amusement, but were productive of very opposite consequences, as the state of the atmosphere might always regulate the portions of exercise necessary to the ends this laborious diversion was originally intended to answer."

What the experts have deducted from the this piece of nonsense is that in the previous couple of days a game of cricket was played between members of the ship Calcutta which reached Port Jackson late in December 1803 and soldiers of one of the army regiments.

And it is also assumed that the game was played on the Town Common, which at that time was the general venue for all games, including the first recorded race horse meeting. Later in October 1810 Governor Macquarie renamed The Common to Hyde Park, a name it still retains.

However, it is highly unlikely that this was the very first game of cricket played in the colony of New South Wales. As indicated in the previous chapter, the Duke of Wellington had seen to it that cricket was a game established in all arms of the British forces.

Given the popularity of the game amongst the soldiers and sailors of the times, it is quite probable that it would have been brought to the new colony much earlier, perhaps with the First Fleet in 1788, with games being played between the different regiments. We just don't know because there were no earlier mentions of the game in print. So 1804 has to be the starting point.

Governor Macquarie's Order changing the name of The Common referred

THE ROLE OF THE ARMY

As recorded in Chapter One the British Army and Navy played a very vital role in spreading the game of cricket out from Britain to the then ever expanding British Empire, and to a few foreign places as well. They also played a leading role fostering the game in the various outposts where they were stationed. And this included Sydney where there was also a very large armed force due to the convicts. Above is a painting by J. Maclehose in 1838 of the Barracks in George Street. Below is an earlier sketch (circa 1820's) showing an actual game of cricket being played in the same Barracks. Most matches of course were between the various Regiments stationed in Sydney at the time and in almost all cases heavy betting was the rule.

Officers indulge in a favourite pastime, a game of cricket, in the grounds of the Military Barracks, Sydney.

to it as an "Exercising Ground", "A Cricket Ground", and "Racecourse". So, by 1810 cricket must have been a well established sport played on the ground.

By the early 1820's various civilian cricket clubs existed in Sydney, as well as the army clubs. After a while some of these clubs moved briefly to the Domain, but finding this unsuitable eventually moved to a paddock in Redfern, which became the home of cricket for many years.

Throughout the 1820's and 1830's the game progressed rapidly into the outer Sydney suburbs and even to small country towns which were springing up both north and south of Sydney, as well as over the Blue Mountains.

For all of this time Sydney dominated the game but gradually it spread first to Tasmania, then to Melbourne, Brisbane and Adelaide. But progress was slow because of the huge distances and lack of transport so inter-city games were not really practical until the 1850's and then only rarely staged.

The gold rushes, which started in 1851, brought in their trail not only vast wealth but huge improvements in land transport through the big coaching companies such as Cobb & Co spreading their routes all over the eastern states making it possible for teams to get around to play distant games. And as time went on the army games fell away to be replaced by well financed civilian clubs who could afford well equipped cricket grounds complete with ornate grandstands. By the 1860's cricket was up and running, especially in Sydney and Melbourne, ready to welcome the first of the visiting English touring teams.

By then a big change had come over the game itself as Sydney no longer was dominant force in cricket. That role was now occupied by Melbourne as they had been the recipient of the great flows of gold into their coffers. And this led to intense rivalry between the two cities, which was a huge blocking force to the game developing into an Australian oriented one, since the two cities seemed to be unable to agree on anything.

The Melbourne Cricket Club was founded in 1838, long before the state of Victoria came into being, and the club first had a ground almost in the heart of Melbourne, close to the Catholic Cathedral in Little Collins

The number of private schools in Australia was not great, but collectively they did much to promote cricket, even those outside the capital cities. This sketch shows a match under way at the Cooerwul Academy, at Bowenfels, N.S.W.

Street, near William Street. Later they moved on to what was then the Richmond Police Paddock, where they built a magnificent ground far surpassing any Sydney grounds.

The first Inter-Colonial match was played in Melbourne on March 26 and 27, 1856 on the Richmond Ground. Initially Melbourne had challenged Sydney to play two matches, one in Sydney and one in Melbourne, each for five hundred pounds. The Sydney-siders declined because they thought that Melbourne had the stronger side. But they agreed to go to Melbourne for a match with no betting involved, solely to promote the game.

On the day the weather was perfect, a German band had been engaged to start the proceedings, and a huge crowd of spectators were present. But the game almost didn't get under way because of a dispute of who was to bat first, one of those ungainly squabbles that kept popping up between the two adversaries.

Sydney claimed the right to bat first under the old law that the team who had traveled the furthest had that right. The Melbourne-ites responded by claiming that old law had long vanished, and that the modern practice was for the two umpires to toss a coin to see who went first. Several players from Sydney threatened to walk out. Things were getting very tense when Sydney gave in and agreed to abide by the modern rules.

The umpires tossed and Melbourne got the call, batting first and making a modest 63 in the first innings and only 28 in the second. Sydney had an easy win with scores of 76 and 16 for seven wickets.

The bad feelings in that first match continued to fester for most of the rest of the century to the great detriment of the game itself. Some of the more memorable clashes will be outlined in later chapters.

Cricket was much slower in evolving in the distant colonies such as South Australia, Western Australia and Queensland because of lack of transport so they had to rely on local club games which did little to upgrade the standard of play. Even the coming of the railways did not help very much, so for the whole rest of the 19th Century the cricket was completely dominated by Sydney and Melbourne.

GAMES PLAYED IN SYDNEY STREETS IN 1846

The out-door games of old England are kept up here with greater observance than in any other colony of my acquaintance. It is amusing and pleasant to see the minor games of the minor people come round in their seasons. In the keen weather of July the hoop has its sway. As a pedestrian spectator—if you preserve a green recollection of your schoolboy days—you criticise with a bland and protective feeling the skilful inch-driving of the urchin's one-wheeled coach; but when, on horseback, you see the emblem of eternity abandoned by its guide just when it most needs his care, wabbling across your path, how differently do you regard this innocent toy and its innocent owner! The weather grows warmer, and the peg-top comes in, followed by marbles—both games of an exciting nature. The earnest little gamblers—for the winner, as you may recollect, pockets a handful of marbles as well as his opponent's "taw"—knuckle down in the middle of the street or pavement, and if you disturb the state of the game—look out, that's all! In the cricket season the male portion of the rising generation are perfectly engrossed in the study of that noble game. Every possible imitation of a wicket forms the target for every possible object that school-boy ingenuity can compel to do duty for a ball. Your milk-boy sets his can down, in open day, for the vegetable lad to have " only just one ball" at it with a turnip; and old women are continually seen scolding and threatening because their legs have, quite accidentally of course, been treated as a set of stumps.

The piece above is an extract from OUR ANTIPODES. Or; Residence and Rambles in the Australasian Colonies, and with glimpses of the Goldfields, published in three volumes in 1852 in London. The author was Lieutenant Colonel Godfrey Charles Mundy, the Deputy Adjutant General for the Australasian forces, which then included New Zealand. Mundy was established in Sydney from early 1846 to late in 1851, and was a keen observer of the minute things in life, including cricket being played by the Sydney urchins.

CHAPTER 4

The Gambling Years

Australia has long been known as one of the world's great gambling nations, a place where the inhabitants have been known to bet on two flies crawling up a wall. Yet the same inhabitants were profoundly shocked in the 1990's when the great gambling scandals broke out in Indian cricket, especially when it became known that a couple of Australian cricketers had been involved by taking thousands of dollars from an Indian bookmaker for supplying information on the weather and the state of the pitches.

The total amounts in the scandal were huge with one Indian bookmaker admitting that he had an annual turnover on cricket bets of thirty million dollars. With such sums involved, corruption was inevitable and the number of score cards that were fakes as a result of players taking bribes must have run into thousands that should have been wiped from the record books of several nations.

What bothered the Australians the most was the dread thought that their cricketers might have been involved in these games of "fixed" cricket matches. "Football match fixing", yeah possible. "Cricket fixing", nah, nah. Aussie cricket was too straight for that. And probably they were right in that assumption.

Yet, had they known their cricket history they would have been aware that in the early days of the game, both in England and Australia, it was riddled with the problem of gambling on cricket matches, including plenty of cases of match rigging in the very early days.

And we have evidence of this going back to the 18th Century in England. As an accompanying illustration of an advertisement for a cricket match in the Kentish Gazette, dated September 6, 1791, for a game the following day between the Gentlemen of Teynham and Linstead against the Gentlemen of Faversham, for one guinea a man, clearly shows.

The practice of playing for money, usually ten or twenty guineas a game,

The advertisement in the Kentish Gazette of September 6, 1791, was for a cricket match to be played the following day at a guinea a player, indicating how gambling was an established part of early cricket.

was common through the towns and villages in the 18th and 19th centuries. In fact it probably was the glue that held the game together in this period.

And when the game came to Australia officially in 1804 as recorded in the previous chapter, there was ample evidence that the good old English practice of linking gambling to cricket had also firmly taken root in the colony, especially in games played between the various Sydney based Army regiments.

The first record of a match between a regimental team and a civilian based side on March 23, 1830, was advertised as Military Officers versus Civilians, and according to the Sydney Monitor some very heavy betting took place on the event, not only for money but a whole batch of items for trade such as maize, butter, sawn timber, pigs, fish and salt. Incidentally, the Civilians won the match by 38 runs.

The Sydney Gazette in October 1839 reported that the 39th Regiment had challenged 57th Regiment to a match of one hundred pounds a side. In 1832 when a match was played on May 7 between the 17th Regiment and the 29th Regiment, the press reported that the stake was three hundred pounds, a very substantial sum in those days.

And as noted in the previous chapter the Melbourne Cricket Club challenged the Sydney Cricket Club to an Inter-Colonial game in 1856 for five hundred pounds a side. The Sydney Club did not accept the challenge because they thought they had the weaker side.

When English teams started to come to Australia from the 1860's they did not play for money directly but most of the matches attracted bookmakers and it was a fairly common sight to see players backing their own side. And further down the track, as we will see later on in this volume, the damage that gambling can cause to the game of cricket.

Both the Sydney and Melbourne cricket clubs, who dominated the game throughout the 19th Century, from time to time, tried to stamp out gambling on the games but it was a losing battle as the bookies usually came out in front.

CHAPTER 5

The First English Tour

For more than half a century cricket in Australia was left to its own devices without help or hindrance from the Mother Country England. From 1861 that changed as a result of intermittent visits by English teams which resulted in higher levels of public enthusiasm for the game and a general raising of standards in the colonies.

The initiative for the first visit in 1861 did not come from the Old Dart. It came through sponsorship by a Melbourne firm of caterers, Spiers & Pond who were then active in catering for large sporting and other events. They viewed such sponsorships as both a practical business venture and a way of advertising their services.

Their original target was Charles Dickens, the noted English author, whose books were best sellers throughout the colonies, but the money they offered was not enough to entice him Down Under for a speaking tour. Rejected by Dickens they turned their attention to the game of cricket whose occasional inter city matches between Sydney and Melbourne were attracting large crowds of spectators.

Spiers & Pond opened negotiations with a leading Surrey player, H.H. Stephenson, offering all players in the team one hundred and fifty pounds, plus all expenses paid. This was a generous offer for the period but the money conscious Yorkshire players, the leading players of the time, rejected it out of hand. As a result Stephenson was only able to cobble together a rather lop sided touring team which included seven Surrey players, H.H. Stephenson (Captain), W. Caffyn, W. Griffith, W. Mortlock, G. Bennett, R. Addison, T. Hearne, T. Sewell, W. Moodie, C. Lawrence, E. Stephenson and G. Wells, (Father of the famous novelist H.G. Wells).

The team arrived in Melbourne on the Great Britain, then the largest ship afloat, on Christmas Eve. Thanks to the substantial publicity efforts of Spiers & Pond the team received a rousing welcome from three thousand people who had gathered on the docks at Port Melbourne, and who stood under the Great Arch that had been erected there. On disembarking the first English team to set foot on Australian soil was driven into town on a specially hired coach pulled by eight grey horses.

No doubt the visitors were impressed at being give treatment usually reserved for Royalty, but a rather sour note was expressed by The Age, then the leading Melbourne daily newspaper, when it printed the following in its Boxing Day edition:

"The game of cricket has no heartier admirers than ourselves, but we imagine from the super abundant effusion which the approaching contest has excited that some tremendous crisis was at hand, or that some trial which is to make us or to mar us for ever is approaching."

No doubt the team members were well entertained over Christmas by their hosts but problems awaited them soon afterwards. They had been hugely impressed by the new Grandstand erected by the Melbourne Cricket Club, a stand seven hundred feet long, said to be the finest in the world, far better than any they had seen in England.

But they were barred from using the ground for practice as from the 26th to the 28th of December the Melbourne Scots were holding a three day Festival there and the Scots were not going to make way for a mere band of English cricketers. Spiers & Pond were catering for the Scot Festival but even they could not pull rank to get the English team admitted to the ground.

Then another problem arose. When the ground became available the English team was asked to play a Melbourne team of 22 a common enough practice in those days. Although the English team had played against 22 players in Canada and New York on the way to Australia, Stephenson objected that this was too much after a long sea voyage and no practice. The press accused them of cowardice in the face of the enemy, and Stephenson even received a white feather in the post. After a somewhat heated debate Stephenson agreed to play against a Melbourne side of 18 players.

The match, when it finally got under way, attracted huge crowds, who must have been disappointed to find that their local champions, all eighteen of them, could not stand up to the onslaught of the two main English bowlers, Griffith and Bennett. The home side collapsed for 118 runs in the first innings and 102 in the second. The Melbourne bowlers did not unduly trouble the visitors who scored a respectable 305, the top scorer being Caffyn with 79.

The match was scheduled for three days but finished in two. To fill in the gap the enterprising Spiers & Bond produced a massive balloon featuring on it's sides large pictures of Queen Victoria and all the members of the English team. It was blown up in the centre of the MCC and rose to seven thousand feet, eventually returning to earth in Albert Street, East Melbourne, no doubt frightening the horses in the vicinity no end.

Spiers & Pond must have realised they were on a winner with the tour as they spared no expense in transporting the team around the Victorian countryside, hiring an impressive leviathan Cobb & Co coach for the purpose, and putting them up in first class hotels.

After the Melbourne victory Stephenson agreed to play all final matches against the odds of 22 players. And they won all but two of the remaining matches. The press was quick to point out that on these two occasions the results may not have been due to lack of cricketing skills but to the fact that the members of the team had imbibed far too much liquor at the lavish pre match luncheons put on before the start of play.

Their greatest win was against a weak Beechworth side. Stephenson's team made an impressive 264, then bundled poor Beechworth out twice for 26 and 56. As it was felt that the big crowd of spectators had not got full value for their entry money something had to be done to fill in the rest of the time that had been allocated. It was decided that the star of the English side, the all rounder Griffith, would on his own, play the entire normal eleven Beechworth side in a one wicket match. He managed to bowl the now very demoralised local side out for one run, a bye, and ten ducks. He then batted and scored two runs and it was all over for the day. The good folk of Beechworth must still have nightmares over the events of that day.

The English side had comfortable wins against Geelong and Ballarat, but lost to Castlemaine, which then erected a plaque proclaiming that it's team was the first to beat an English team on Victorian soil – no doubt with the aid of some liquor in the pre-match lunch.

After the triumphal Victorian tour the team moved on to Sydney when they had their second loss of the tour against a 22 man side containing both Sydney and Melbourne players.

After that the team sailed back to England, each member carrying his one hundred and fifty pound bonus. Spiers & Pond must have been laughing all the way to the bank as they made a clear profit of eleven thousand pounds out of the tour, a factor that enabled them to up anchor and return to England, from which they originally came, to explore new catering enterprises in their homeland, to the great loss of Melbourne.

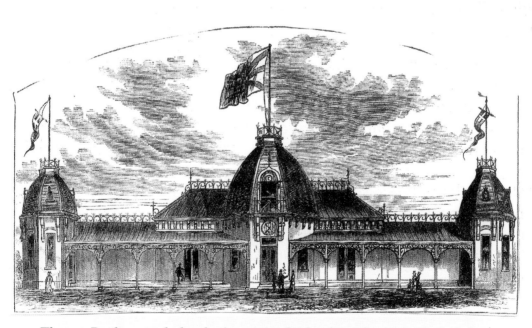

The new Pavilion attached to the Association Cricket Ground at Moore Park, Sydney, 1870's thanks to the Gold Rush money.

THE RICHMOND CRICKET GROUND, MELBOURNE, IN 1864

I will have to introduce a personal note on this item. Every day when I enter my home office I am delighted to be faced with the above scene, properly framed of course. It is one of the scarce hand coloured lithographs sized 27 x 37 cm produced by Charles Trodel, of Melbourne, in 1864. I acquired it some years ago from an auction in Melbourne who quite obviously didn't have any knowledge of what they were offering, for a mere thirty dollars. At the time I knew it was a bargain but I was somewhat stunned to find out that an identical item had realised $3450 at a Melbourne Christies Auction in June 1999.

The subject of the work is the Richmond Cricket Ground owned by the Melbourne Cricket Club mentioned in the last chapter but updated since then, the old grandstand being demolished and replaced by a larger new one, with three refreshment booths and private viewing boxes.

And the actual scene shown is the first day's play on January I, 1864, of the first match played by George Parr's visiting team, against a Victorian side. The Victorians made 145 and 143 in their two innings, and the English team made 176 in their first innings and late on the second day were only nine runs short of victory when at precisely six o'clock the umpires took the bails off and declared the match a very controversial draw.

So the object is not only a very pleasing piece of colonial art to view, but it is also part of Australian Cricket History. And as my copy came from a Blackham source it was probably once owned by t John Blackham, the greatest wicketkeeper in the world in the 19th Century. All this for a meagre thirty dollars – you certainly can be lucky sometimes in life!

CHAPTER 6

The Second English Tour

What must have impressed the English Cricket Establishment about Stephenson's 1861-2 tour was the enormous profit of eleven thousand pounds made by the sponsors Spiers & Pond. No doubt in anticipation of being able to match these figures a second tour was organised for the 1863-4 season, this one being sponsored from the English end.

The second tour was led by the noted Notts player George Parr and had an itinerary very similar to the Stephenson tour. All the games were to be played against Australian teams of 18 and 22 players. And they emerged from the tour without losing a single game – perhaps they were a more sober team than the first one!

But they failed to attract the big crowds that had flocked to Stephenson's team, partly because the novelty of a visiting team had worn off a bit but mainly because the flair for the publicity that Spiers & Pond had been able to generate was lacking this time round.

However, the Parr tour had a very important bonus that could not have foreseen at the time. Included in the tour was the well known English all rounder Charles Lawrence, the only player who had also been a member of Stephenson's team of 1861-2.

His first tour must have made a great impression on him because after the Parr tour ended he stayed behind and settled in Australia, having a great impact on the cricketing history of his new home. And he was in due course the pivotal player in leading the very first Australian team to England - the famous Aboriginal tour of 1868 which is the subject of the next chapter.

CHAPTER 7

The Aboriginal Tour

As a result of the first two English touring teams visiting the western districts of Victoria, the aborigines of that area became very interested in cricket and soon demonstrated skills in the game, especially bowling.

As related in the last chapter, Charles Lawrence, who had been a member of both the first and second English touring side stayed behind and settled in Australia at the conclusion of the second tour.

He took a keen interest in the talents of the western district aborigines and began coaching them. He was assisted in this endeavour by a former Devonshire cricketer, W.R. Hayman and an Australian, Thomas Wentworth Spencer Wills, who had a strange and tragic life.

Wills was born in 1835 in New South Wales into a wealthy grazing family. He was sent to Rugby School in England where he excelled in sport, playing football and captaining the school Cricket Eleven. In the 1853-6 period he became a star player for Kent and for the Marylebone Cricket Club. When he returned to Australia in 1856 he became one of the star players for the Melbourne Cricket Club. A big hitter as a batsman, he was also a major bowler and introduced round – arm bowling to Australian cricket.

In 1861 he helped his family establish a new property at Cullinlaringo, some 250 miles west of Rockhampton.

In October 1861, while Thomas and his younger brother Cedric, were absent from the property, a band of aborigines who had attached themselves to the settlement, and who were regarded as harmless, suddenly attacked the white occupants, killing them all, the worst massacre of whites in the history of pioneer settlements of Australia. The two surviving Wills brothers joined a large expedition of police and other settlers in tracking down and killing the offending aborigines.

Thomas stayed on the property for a year, working it with Cedric, then departed forever, leaving it all to his brother who remained on the property for the rest of his life.

Thomas returned to Victoria where he became a coach, helping Lawrence and Hayman train the aborigines in the Lake Wallace region, a remarkable act considering he confrontation with the aborigines in Queensland. But he never spoke of these events, even to close friends.

Wills later returned to Melbourne to live where he helped draw up the rules for a new football code – Australian Rules. He played in this game, mainly for Geelong, playing in 210 games before retiring in 1876. His final years were full of tragedy due to heavy drinking, and he committed suicide on May 2, 1880.

By 1866 coaches Lawrence and Hayman thought their aboriginal players were sufficiently advanced to start playing major cricket. They formed an all-aboriginal team which they sent out to various villages and towns to play the locals. They played with such success that there was talk of them being sent to England and very soon a possible backer for the idea appeared on the horizon.

Unfortunately he turned out to be a "dud" of the first orders, if not an outright conman. His name was Captain W.E.B. Gurnettt, who posed as a man of substance, but in fact lived in a boarding house at 219 Macquarie Street, Sydney. He had grand ideas for the tour which he proposed for the aboriginal team, but he failed to produce tickets for the ship bookings he said had been made, and his cheques started bouncing all over the place.

Hayman who had taken his team to Sydney in expectation of departing from there was forced to call the whole venture off and return the disgruntled and unhappy black warriors back to their western district homes. Hayman claimed to have been out of pocket by four hundred pounds from the tragedy of 1867.

However, out of the ashes of defeat their arose another, much more reliable champion, their old friend Charles Lawrence, who was now a successful Sydney hotelier, accompanied by George Smith, a former Lord Mayor of Sydney, and a shadowy figure, a Sydney businessman W.G. Graham, who jointly agreed to sponsor a visit to England starting early in 1868.

With new heart, Hayman set about organising a new team for the venture, a number of the original team having died or withdrawn from the contest. And the new entrepreneurs faced some problems getting the trip off the ground as they had to fend off efforts by the Central Board for the Protection of Aborigines trying to stop the event (They failed because they found they didn't have the necessary powers to prevent it) and a concerted campaign by a Sydney physician, Dr W.T. Molloy, who wrote a string of letters to newspapers alleging that the aborigines on the team would suffer all sorts of illnesses from foreign diseases and that they would be exploited unmercifully by the promoters of the tour.

All these attempts failed and the team eventually sailed from Sydney on February 8, 1868, on the Parramatta. Charles Lawrence was the only white member of the team and he went as Captain. Because the aborigines all had long unpronounceable native names they were all assigned common English names, and the team comprised the following players: Johnny Mullagh, Johnny Cuzens, Bullocky, Red Cap, Twopenny, King Cole, Tiger, Dick-a-Dick, Peter, Charley, Mosquito, Jim Crow and Sundown.

The team had all been dressed in common outfits of white cream trousers, and brilliant red shirts and sashes, and individually coloured caps. They made quite a display when lined up for the cameras of the day.

The English cricketing Establishment didn't know what to make of this strange bunch of cricketers that had suddenly arrived on their doorstep seeking matches against English teams. The MCC decided to completely ignore this weird assembly. And the county teams followed suit, resulting in the team having to arrange matches in small towns and villages where the response was much more friendly.

In fact they made quite an impact in the countryside as apart from their cricket skills they also performed with boomerangs and displayed aboriginal artefacts and put on ceremonial displays after matches. Because of this, and the fact that they did not belong to established (whiter) teams back in Australia, the English Establishment regarded them as more of a circus than a visiting cricket team and simply ignored the whole event. But out in the countryside they were much more than this. Their manner and behaviour was impeccable and they proved to be wonderful ambassadors for Australia and for their aboriginality.

But they had a lot to contend with, apart from the official apathy. That summer proved to be exceptionally wet and cold and this took a heavy toll on the players. One of the team, King Cole, was laid low and died, while two other team members, Jim Crow and Sundown, became so ill they had to be returned home early.

The team had a very tough schedule of two, and sometimes three, matches each week, but they managed to engage in 47 matches. They won 14 and lost 14, the rest being either drawn or washed out by rain.

Johnny Mullagh emerged as the star of the tour having scored 1700 runs at an overall average of 23, while at the same time taking 257 wickets, each at a cost of 10. A very remarkable record in any circumstances. Johnny Cuzens was the only other player to turn in high figures, scoring over 1000 runs and taking 114 wickets.

So ended the first Australian cricket tour of England. The sponsors of the tour covered expenses but did not make the profits they had anticipated. There was no great welcome home for them back in Melbourne and most of the team faded back into their station hand activities in Western Victoria without making any further contribution to cricket history.

Only Johnny Mullagh followed up with any sort of cricket career. On his return from England he was appointed as a professional coach but Melbourne life didn't suit him and he returned to station life in the western districts where he played in local matches. The only time he played in a Victorian team was in a match against the 1879 Lord Harris team when he top scored with 36 in the second Victorian innings. In his later years he worked as a rabbiter on a western district property and it was there in a camp hut that he died in August 1891.

The Aboriginal tour started out with great hopes which were never really attained due mainly by the boycott by the sniffy English Cricket Establishment. Which is a shame because the young aborigines involved had much to offer with a bit of encouragement, and they certainly pioneered the way from Australia to England long before their White counterparts.

The lack of support they received from the White Cricket Establishment in Australia was perhaps typical of the period, but it certainly isn't anything the Melbourne Cricket Club can boast about.

W.G.GRACE.

Dr W.G. Grace was the foremost English cricket player of the late 19th Century and early 20th Century. He first came to Australia in the 1873-4 season on his now famous Honeymoon Tour. He ran into all sorts of trouble, especially with some unworldly Cornish Moonta copper miners in South Australia. The story of the tour is a great read.

CHAPTER 8

The Honeymoon Tour

If the gentlemen of the Marylebone Cricket Club regarded the Aboriginal tour of England a bit of a joke, as the sideline to a circus really, they would have taken an entirely different attitude to the third English tour of Australia in 1873-4.

This was because it was led by "one of their own" the redoubtable Dr. W.G. Grace, the greatest cricketer of the 19th Century. Yet, in its way, this tour was much more like a circus than any displays by the Aboriginal tour some five years earlier.

William Gilbert Grace (1848-1915) was only 25 and newly married when he embarked on his first overseas venture leading a team to Australia. And he took his bride with him turning it into cricket's first , and possibly only, "Honeymoon Tour" - a tour of continual conflict and gossip, mainly due to Grace's fiery temperament.

For a start, he got everyone offside by demanding the unheard fee of fifteen hundred pounds plus all expenses, and he was supposed to be one of the Gentlemen amateurs of the game. The Australian cricketing bodies sponsoring the tour eventually agreed to this brigandage because of Grace's pulling power with his fans.

And within the team there was constant seething discontent by the Professionals who had to travel second class and put up with inferior accommodation while the Amateurs, the so-called Gentleman players, always went first class and stayed at the best hotels.

Right from the start of the tour the Australian newspapers, one and all, branded Grace as an over-bearing Captain and a bumptious individual who antagonised everyone he met. In good old fashioned Australian egalitarian style they set about giving this Pommy upstart "Tall Poppy" a hard time. And they succeeded.

Admittedly the good doctor had a lot to contend with, apart from the

Because of his bulk, and his unusually sharp temper, Dr Grace was a sitting target for the cartoonists of England and Australia. But this cartoon of him was a rather friendly one as it was sketched by one of his close friends, Max Beerbohm. It first appeared in the London Daily Telegraph in 1895.

constant sniping from the Professionals in his own team. The Australian summer heat was almost unbearable to tender English skins, while some of the pitches they had to play on were beyond description. And Grace's temper was not improved by the fact that the team was losing some of the games as a result of excessive drinking, sometimes brazenly on the fields, by some of his rebellious Professionals.

After a relatively civilised match against a Melbourne Cricket Club team Grace and his men had to venture out into the Victorian countryside as earlier teams had done. To face up to sometimes hostile rural crowds and sometimes some incredible playing pitches, contrasting a lot with the calm and peaceful village playing fields of Old England.

After a relatively easy match at Ballarat, where the team trounced the home side with a score of 470 (Grace with 126 and his younger brother 112), they had to endure a twelve hour bone jolting journey in an ancient Cobb & Co coach to Stawell. When Grace was taken to the field to inspect the pitch he asked where the wicket was, and was told he was standing on it. A Melbourne paper reported that the ground was as rough as ploughed field and the wicket itself was as hard as iron. Stawell won the match by one run.

But more wonders were ahead. The South Australian Cricket Association was anxious for Grace and his men to visit Adelaide for a match but were horrified when Grace demanded a fee of eight hundred pounds. They were still dithering about whether to accept or reject these terms, when out of the blue Grace received an offer from another South Australian club.

This came from an unlikely source, the Kadina Cricket Club. The Adelaide people were outraged at having been sidelined this way, especially as they had not heard of the Kadina Cricket Club. Which was not surprising since no such club had existed until that day. It was invented on the spot by a group of Cornish miners at the nearby Moonta copper mines.

Not only did they not have a properly instituted club, but they had no team or cricket ground – though Grace was not aware of any of these inconvenient facts when he accepted their offer to play a match for eight hundred pounds.

But what the Moonta men lacked in essentials they made up for it in enthusiasm and community spirit. As soon as they received Dr Grace's telegram of acceptance they set about rectifying some of the obvious deficiencies.. They organised working bees and quickly had produced a sort of cricket ground in an open paddock, complete with not one but two fairly shaky grandstands, and they entirely surrounded the ground with a seven foot high fence to prevent freeloaders enjoying the coming event – Kadina's very first cricket match.

The men of Kadina had worked minor miracles approaching that of the loaves and fishes act, but there were some flaws in their master plan as they had little knowledge of the basics of the cricket field.

When Grace and his team arrived and inspected the field they could not believe their eyes. The entire surface of the ground was covered in small gravel and when Grace looked around for a wicket on this grassless wilderness he couldn't find one, the locals being unaware that cricket grounds came supplied with a wicket.

Grace decided they would have to make the best of it as one place was as bad as any other. Finally he selected a spot but found the ground so hard that the stumps refused to make entry so water had to be brought to soften up the ground before the game could commence.

All 22 members of the home side had been kitted out in sparkling new white flannels, but it was clear from the start that they had never played a game of cricket before and they had no idea what they were supposed to do either with bat or ball. The correspondent of The Australasian summed it all up neatly in his report of the match:

"It was impossible to describe the play for the simple reason that there was no play to describe. Many victims would not believe they were out and it afforded considerable merriment to the cognoscenti to hear men appealing when clean bowled. The crudeness of their ideas about cricket was wonderful to behold."

The home side batted first and managed to chalk up a total of 42, the top score being sundries with 8. Grace's team didn't fare much better on an almost unplayable ground but got to 64.

However, it was in the second innings that the Kadina team was destined to go into the record books of cricket history. Not learning from the mistakes of the first innings, they were dismissed for a grand total of 13, of which 5 were sundries, and there were fifteen ducks. Some records were also chalked up on the English bowling side as McIntyre finished with seven wickets for one run, while Lillywhite had 13 wickets for seven runs.

While all this was taking place telegrams were being exchanged between Dr Grace and the committee of the South Australian Cricket Association trying to save something from their procrastination that allowed the Kadina Club to steal the English team from under their nose. The upshot was that Grace agreed to play a three day match in Adelaide starting the next day.

The Kadina team was hugely upset by this arrangement. They had been trounced on the field after paying eight hundred pounds for the privilege of being the only South Australian club to play the English team, and now they had lost this exclusivity to Adelaide. They threatened legal action, but Dr Grace stood firm.

This also threw a distinct cloud over the big banquet they had arranged for that evening, an event that by tradition would go on for most of the night. Dr Grace and his men would have to leave on a coach departing from Kadina at nine o'clock to reach Adelaide by starting time of 2pm the next day. The result was that the banquet had to end early with recriminations all round from the angry locals. It would be a long time before Kadina staged another cricket match.

For Dr Grace and his men the long coach tour to Adelaide was another cross they had to bear. They reached Adelaide on schedule but it was a tired and emotional team that took to the field at 3pm. It could not be said that they played with their usual enthusiasm but they did manage to chalk up innings of 108 and 76 against the Adelaide teams more modest 65 and 82.

It was not an inspiring game and was remembered in local cricket circles only for one incident. That was when Dr Grace made a mighty stroke sending the ball on its way to what seemed a certain six only to have a member of the fielding side, Alexander Crooks, lean back over the

WICKET KEEPER: "Owzat?"

Dr. GRACE: "Not out. I've just declared this a No Ball."

boundary ropes to take an incredible one handed catch.

At the time Crooks was a lowly bank clerk with the Commercial Bank but the dismissal of the mighty Dr Grace earned him such publicity that he earned quick promotion and eventually ended up as General Manager of the Bank of South Australia. Alas, the story does not have a happy ending as his banking efforts failed to measure up to his cricket skills, and he was later dismissed when under his control the bank chalked up losses of a million pounds.

The final match of Dr Grace's tour was not without its controversial side. This was against a New South Wales side in Sydney, a game that attracted a huge crowd of fairly partisan spectators.

The match began badly for the visiting team when in the first over Dr Grace had his middle stump knocked over. The good doctor took this minor setback in his stride and dealt with it in his usual style. Declaring that the large crowd had come to see him bat, he declared the offensive delivery a "No Ball" and took his stance at the wicket. The nonplussed umpire let him get away with this cheeky decision to the cheers of the crowd, and play resumed as if nothing special had happened. The incident received a lot of comment in the press and the cartoonists had a field day with it including the carton shown on the opposite page.

Dr Grace then took his bride and his rebellious team back to England. What Mrs Grace thought of the tour unfortunately does not appear to be on public record, which is a pity because they don't make honeymoons like that any more and her observations of the event would surely have made interesting reading.

James Lillywhite brought the fourth English touring side to Australia in 1877 which had the distinction of being the first English team to play an all-Australian side, thus creating the later named Test series. While the planning for this was underway he took his team off to New Zealand where he lost his wicket keeper in a very unusual manner. The complete story of which is told here for the first time.

CHAPTER NINE

The Lillywhite Tour

In 1877 James Lillywhite, the star bowler in Dr Grace's unhappy tour, brought the fourth English touring team to Australia. Lillywhite was an around arm slow bowler of uncanny accuracy, with a very smart mind which enabled him to think batsmen out by studying their weak spots.

He also appeared to be a smart leader of men. As his team comprised only Professionals, the result was more harmony since everyone was treated alike in matters of travel and accommodation. And his team made cricket history by being the first English team to play joint Australian teams in what later became Test Matches.

But his team also was destined to play a different type of cricket history which he would very much have preferred to escape when over in New Zealand he "lost" his wicketkeeper, who became embroiled in a gambling affray which ended up in two inconvenient court cases.

But all this was in the future. On arrival in Australia it took a while to adjust to the local conditions and they lost matches to several strong Victorian and New South Wales sides.

This prompted writers in several newspapers to suggest that they should play even side games against combined Victorian and New South Wales sides so the matches could be advertised as England versus Australia. The other states had to be left out of these Australian sides because of travel difficulties.

For once the Melbourne and Sydney cricket authorities seemed to agree that this was a sensible idea. No doubt this was prompted by thoughts of all the extra gate takings that would be generated by such matches. They agreed to stage a couple of such matches but needed time to work out all the differing state points that would inevitably be involved.

So while the states were dickering over these negotiations, Lillywhite took his team off for a tour of New Zealand, starting at Auckland and then working their way down to the South Island. All went well until they arrived in Christchurch where they struck trouble on a major scale.

The culprit was Edward Pooley, their wicketkeeper, who was a bit of a con man who believed implicitly in Barnum's theory on mugs, namely that one is born every minute. And Pooley evidently believed it was his duty to relieve such mugs of as much of their spare change as he could. And he had a well oiled plan of how to do this.

His plan was to go into a busy bar on the day before a match, talk very loud and boastfully as to how he had a unique talent for guessing what every batsman would score in a match in both innings. And he was prepared to take bets on it.

In the bar of the Commercial Hotel in Cathedral Square, where the team was staying, he found the perfectly mathematically challenged Kiwi, one Ralph Donkin, an elderly retired surveyor, who was a permanent resident in the hotel.

To enquirers Pooley's pitch went something like this: If anyone wanted to bet on his system he would get someone to write down the names of all the players in next days match, the locals and visiting team players. When this was done he would place two figures against each name, namely the scores they would make in each innings next day. For every innings that he got wrong he would pay out a shilling, and for everyone that he got right the bettor would pay him a pound.

On the surface it looked like a 20 to one odds bet, but it was far more than that as Pooley had knowledge up his sleeve the casual bar follower of the game lacked.

Donkin was one of these casual followers and he fell for the spin. And what was more he convinced three of his mates to join him in a bet so very suddenly Pooley found himself with four victims. A nice haul for such a scam.

After the bets were placed, Pooley persuaded someone in the bar to write down all the names of the players the next day and these totaled 29, 11 for the touring side and 18 for the locals, since this was an against the odds match. With two innings that meant Pooley had to come up with 58 separate numbers. Pooley simply wrote two noughts against each name which meant he was betting on 58 ducks.

Most of the patrons in the bar were puzzled by this and they couldn't figure out what the catch was. They didn't wake up to the fact that Pooley's maximum liability was only 58 shillings (two pounds 18 shillings) which meant that there had to be only three ducks in the match at a pound a piece and he was in front. And what he did know was that the grounds of these matches were so rough to play on that ducks almost always featured high on the list of every match.

At some stage Donkin must have smelt the odour of a very large rat, or he and his mates may have gone out and done some sums. He came back and confronted Pooley, claiming the whole thing was a scam (he was right there) and he said all bets were off. Pooley refused this request and said he and his mates had to stick to the rules of such matters. Lots of bad language followed and this lasted all the evening, so everyone went to bed in a sour mood that night.

In the match the next day there were eleven ducks which meant that after deducting the 47 wrong answers at a shilling each (two pounds seven shillings) had to be deducted from the eleven pounds due on the ducks, namely a net payout of nine pounds and thirteen shillings on each bet, a total due on the four bets of thirty eight pounds and twelve shilling.

When Donkin refused to pay up Pooley accused him of being a welsher and a very heated argument followed, resulting in violence when Donkin hit Pooley across the face and his hand with his heavy walking stick. Blood was flowing freely so Pooley was taken into the hotel and patched up. His injuries were pretty serious as they put him out of action for the rest of the tour of New Zealand.

The hostility between Donkin and his mates and Pooley and some of his team mates, continued throughout the evening and at one stage Pooley lunged over the shoulder of a barman with his good arm and struck Donkin in the face. Donkin fell back but no blood flowed so the blow could not have caused much damage.

Late that night Pooley followed Donkin up to his room and allegedly said that if Donkin slept in his bed that night he wouldn't wake up in the morning. Pooley later denied this but he must have said something serious because Donkin took the hint and slept somewhere else that night.

During the night someone broke into Donkin's now empty room, scattered his clothes all around the room and removed some old sketches from his work days. When Donkin returned in the morning he had a mess to clean up and his two suspects were Pooley and Allen Bramhall, the tour money man, who had helped Pooley out with his scam and whose room was next door to Donkin.

Police were called in to investigate the matter but took no action, saying that concrete evidence was lacking, and that it was a civil matter. Donkin immediately took summonses out against both Pooley and Bramhall.

The team left Christchurch for Dunedin that day with the matter unresolved. Pooley could not play either in the Dunedin or Invercargill matches because of his injured hand. When the team left Invercargill for Melbourne both Pooley and Bramhall stayed behind to face the legal music, though it would have been easy for them to dodge this as there would have been little likelihood of Donkin getting them back from Australia on such slim evidence.

Probably Pooley realized that this would have left him open to continual unwelcome publicity in the future with the charges hanging over his head. Both he and Bramhall returned to Christchurch after the ship had sailed and waited for the wheels of justice to grind slowly on.

In April Pooley appeared in the Magistrates Court where he was cleared on the charge of assaulting Donkin, but he copped a fine of five pounds for using extreme language in public.

The pair still had to face the more serious charges of break and enter and steal to be heard in the Supreme Court. Eventually this was heard by Mr. Justice Johnston, over several days. Early in the piece Justice Johnston concluded that the evidence against Bramhall was negligible and he said he would instruct the jury to discharge him. Evidently the evidence against Pooley was a bit stronger as he allowed this to go the jury, which promptly acquitted both him and Bramhall.

So ended a pretty ridiculous pair of court cases brought on by a pompous

Kiwi out of spite, and where he was as much to blame as his two opponents.

The only winner from all this seems to have been the Lyttleton Times, the leading Christchurch newspaper, which devoted many columns of space to the unusual story over several months, and no doubt increasing its circulation as a result. If nothing else, its readers certainly got a lot of useful information on the dangers of betting on cricket matches.

The villain of the piece himself, Edward Pooley,
bit of a con man, whose gambling scheme backfired
and got him into all sorts of strife.

A sketch of an English bowler playing in the very first test match between England and Australia.

CHAPTER 10

The First Test Matches

When Lillywhite's team sailed from Invercargill to Melbourne they were really sailing into cricket history as the two games they played against a combined Victorian and New South Wales side are counted as being the first Test Matches between England and Australia although the term "Tests" was not applied until sometime later.

And, as noted in the last chapter, they arrived for the first match without one of their key players, the wicketkeeper Edward Pooley. But this calamity paled into insignificance against the one faced by the Australian side who found themselves without the two best bowlers in Australia, Frederick Spofforth, who was undoubtedly the best bowler in the world in the 19th Century, and Frank Allan. It was comparable to an Australian side in the 1980's being asked to face up to England without Lillee and Thomson.

And the loss of Spofforth came about as a direct result of the intense rivalry between Melbourne and Sydney. Negotiations to get the games off the ground were no holds barred affairs with each side having to give way on some issues. The decision to hold both games in Melbourne was hard for Sydney to accept but they had to acknowledge that Melbourne had the better grounds and facilities for such an event.

To compensate for this, Victoria eventually agreed that Sydney should field six players and Melbourne five and that the team should be led by the New South Wales Captain Dave Gregory. Even the Melbournians had to grudgingly admit he was the best man for the job.

But Spofforth, the star New South Wales fast bowler, threw a huge spanner in the works when John Blackham, who Victorians claimed was the world's best wicketkeeper, was chosen for that role. Spofforth immediately had a major hissy fit, claiming that his success was entirely due to the New South Wales keeper, William Murdoch. He flatly declined to play if Murdoch was not chosen. Gregory showed great courage in backing Blackham for the job, whereupon Spofforth withdrew from the team, greatly reducing its chances of success.

The team was then dealt another whammy when the Victorian star bowler Frank Allan announced that he would not be available. He worked for the Victorian Lands Department at Warrnambool, and the Warrnambool Fair, which he claimed he had to attend, was on at the same time as the first game. Allan was hotly assailed in the Melbourne press and someone sent him a white feather, but he stood his ground.

With Australia's two best bowlers missing the home side chances seemed pretty slim, even if the English side lacked their wicketkeeper. The match was played over four days, March 15-18, at the Melbourne Club Cricket Ground before record crowds who turned up for this 'Special Game' but in the end it turned out to be a 'one man' event.

And that man was Charles Bannerman, sometimes described as the Don

C. BANNERMAN

Bradman of the 19th Century. He turned the match into an amazing batting display by making 165 not out in the first innings, only retiring after a rising ball from Ullyet struck him on the hand, splitting a finger open. It was a phenomenal score as no other Australian made more than twenty. It took the total score to a match winning 245.

England replied with a hefty 196. In the second innings Bannerman, with his hands strongly bandaged, made only four runs, and the side was all out for 104. In the second innings England could only muster 108, meaning that Australia had won the first Test Match against England.

The joy and rejoicing throughout the land was enormous and the Melbourne Argus launched a fund for Bannerman ("even though he came from Sydney") which raised one hundred and sixty five pounds- a pound a run. The Melbourne Punch was also ecstatic and burst into rhyme:

There came a tale to England,
'Twas of a contest done:
Australian youths in cricket fields
Had met the cracks and won
They fell like leaves in autumn
Despite old-world dodges
Their efforts vain the runs to gain
Off Kendall or off Hodges
The rose a chant Australia
That echoed to the main.
'Twas confident not "blowing"
"Again we'll do the same".

Alas for the Punch bard, the victory was not to be repeated, at least for some time to come as in the second test played a fortnight later, England won by four wickets. The Melbourne press offered their congratulations to the visitors while the Melbourne Punch failed to burst into rhyme on this occasion.

But the general feeling was that the Australian team had done extremely well handicapped by not having its two best bowlers available and opinion was strong that perhaps on English soil they might get another victory.

The climate had been established for sending the first White team to England to take on the Poms, and everyone seemed to think that Dave Gregory was the right man for the job.

THE CENTENARY OF THE FIRST TEST MATCH

Shown below is the se-tenant strip of six stamps issued in 1977 by the Australian Post Office to mark the Centenary of the first Cricket Test between Australia and England played in Melbourne 1877. The six overlapping designs attempted to show the state of play, but they were not greeted with much enthusiasm by modern cricketers, or by stamp collectors.

One of the latter, Stuart Ross, of Croydon, Victoria, submitted to Stamp News, of which I was then the Editor and Publisher, a somewhat revised version of the Test designs. In the second panel from the left a big hitter was shown hefting a ball out of the grounds for six. The would be designer explained that this was a symbol for one of Kerry Packer's then outlawed players giving the heave ho to the Board of Control.

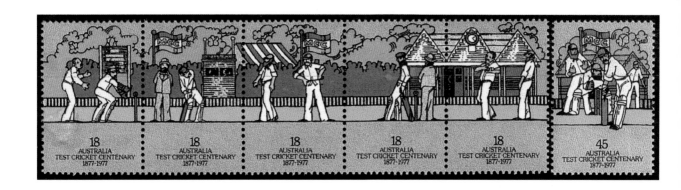

There's gold
Them thar hills
I'll wager

And the Old Codger was dead right about that. There was Gold in them thar hills. Plenty of it. And from 1851 the Gold Rushes were on in almost every state of the colony and the money gushed forth in such volumes that by the end of the Century Australia could claim to have the highest standard of living in the world. The new century brought diminished flows of the stuff, a Great Depression and two world wars to wreck the economy. But the last half of the 19th Century saw all sorts excesses, and nowhere was this more apparent was in the fashion for huge ornate trophies for every sport in the land, including cricket. The two shown on this page are typical for large and small events. Most of these old trophies have long been assigned to the rubbish dumps of the nation but occasionally they pop up at modern auctions for hefty sums of money.

GENTLEMEN v PROFESSIONALS

In the 1870's a new issue raised its ugly head and further divided the two cities of Melbourne and Sydney, namely the question of payments to players. Up to them the issue had been disguised by the payment of "expenses" to help players who did not have independent incomes. But the coming to Australia of English teams containing Professionals, who lived off their cricket earnings, opened up the whole issue. In England the issue fitted nicely into their overall class system, but things were different in the Australia egalitarian attitudes.

The issue was brought into the open by the large cartoon on the opposite page from a Melbourne magazine. Titled TRUE COLOURS the cartoon sets out the Melbourne case for the Gentleman only approach. The batch of tall players on that side of the flag come from the Melbourne Cricketing Association and the mat they are standing on I is labelled Gentlemen Members.

On the other side of pole the flag is flying for the Professional Players who take a share of gate money (so the flag says).

The issue was never resolved in the 19th Century covered by this volume, and no doubt the Gentlemen of Melbourne would have been very upset indeed at the thought of present day system where, at least at the top levels of playing, they are ALL Professionals earning huge amounts of money for their services, with no Gentlemen at all on show at the wickets.

This old postcard produced by the MCC shows Ladies of Rochester game against the Ladies of Maidstone in July 1838. Note the long dresses.

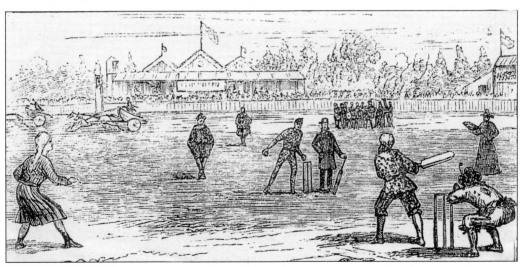

A mixed sexes cricket game being played at Moore Park ground, Sydney, in the 1880's showing the women in very mixed dresses while in the background is a Roman Chariot Race in progress.

CHAPTER 11

The Feminine Invasion

Before we proceed to the remarkable Gregory story, let us pause for moment to consider the feminine invasion of the cricket field which started away back in the 18th Century amongst what Sir Rowland Hill was later to describe as the "Industriously idle ladies of England."

These were the women of the middle and upper classes of England, then starting to enjoy some freedom and always looking around for new fields to conquer.

Perhaps the best example of this came in the shape of Elizabeth, the Countess of Derby, who is shown on a painting attributed to T.H., playing cricket with her lady friends, not a male in sight, in 1779 on the grounds of the great Derby Estate near Epsom.

At the time she was causing great scandal in the Upper Class world by having an affair with a noted rake John Frederick Sackville, third Duke of Dorset, who had been educated at Westmaster School, the acknowledged leading cricket school in the nation, and maintained a life long passion for the game both as a player and supporter. Amongst the many maidens he bowled over on and off the field was the enchantingly beautiful Countess of Derby, much to the dismay of her cuckolded husband who complained in vain of the affair.

In 1790 the Duke married, at the age of forty five, and settled down to pursuits other than cricket. And no doubt by then the Countess of Derby had found other interests to fill her day.

The next pictorial example we have of ladies' cricket was many years later in 1838 when a painting in oils by an unknown artist turned up showing a match between the Ladies of Rochester and the Ladies of Maidestone.

Another interesting example of a women's cricket match came in an early 20th Century advertisement for Elliman's Universal Embrocation showing a woman bowler making a delivery whilst exclaiming "It I will

The Grocers' Picnic at Botany, in the 1880's, a mixed sexes cricket game

have or I will have none."

Australian women came to the cricket scene much later than their English counterparts for the simple reason that in the first half century of settlement there were very few "industriously idle ladies" around the place. The vast number of women convicts were either locked up in the Parramatta Factory or were out working on farms or homes as unpaid labour. The few non-convict women had other things to keep them fully occupied in a busy growing colony.

But in time they, too, started to show an interest in cricket, though pictorial evidence of this activity is scarce. A cartoon in The Sydney Mail of the early 1870's shows two women on the field in a male cricket match, one in traditional long dress to the ground and the other, a younger woman, showing a scandalous amount of leg for the time, while in the background a chariot race is in progress. The event was part of the birthday celebrations of Queen Victoria. A later drawing of 1883 shows in some detail a mixed male/ female match at the Grocers' Picnic at Botany.

However, in 1887 a move was afoot to provide the women of Australia with a cricket-like game of their own to be called Frisquet (or Ladies Cricket). The originator of this rather weird idea was a well known Sydney cricket identity, F.J. Ironside, who a year later was to win some sort of acclaim as author of The Australian Cricketing Handbook.

An interview with Ironside published in a Sydney magazine of the time claimed that two matches of this new Frisquet game had already been played on a ground at Moore Park. Alas, for Ironside's bid for fame in the feminist chronicles, Frisquet seems to have sunk without trace. Perhaps a reading of the complicated rules as outlined in the magazine, will explain why the good ladies of Sydney turned their backs on the whole affair. Below is the full report on the game:

FRISQUET, OR LADIES' CRICKET

This new and original game by Mr F. Ironside, bearing the euphonious name of Frisquet, was augmented some few Sundays since by an opening match, the players being a chosen few. The piece of ground selected for

Women's cricket must have been well advanced by the 1880's for them to attract advertisers.
This shows a female bowler saying as she delivered the ball "It I will have, or I will have none",
the "It" being Ellmans Embrocation.

the purpose was that formerly known as Farmer's, at Moore Park, now unsuited to the purpose of cricket, owing to some portion of the field having been taken in for a plantation.

Being found particularly well adapted to this game (36 x 21 yards being the amount of space required) application has been made by Mr Ironside to the municipal authorities for its use, and in return for his endevours as originator we doubt not that this will be successful. Two matches have already been played, and if the interest of those who have taken part may be taken as any criterion, there is no reason to doubt of its becoming very popular.

As most of our lady readers may sooner or later be interested, we give an outline of the game so that they may, if anxious, prepare themselves to the skill necessary to become good players. We would first repeat that there is nothing of which the lady of the most refined taste could possibly find fault. Married, as well as single, may find pleasure in it, without the fatiguing activity required in rounders and lawn tennis. No exertion is involved exceeding what was stated to be beneficial by Professor Goergs in a lecture at the Riviere College, Woollahra, a few evenings since, on the importance attached by the Greek philosophers to healthy exercises by both men and women, and of the importance of these exercises as preventives to liver complaints and spinal and nervous affections.

Sides being selected (two twelves) the procedure is as in cricket, with the exception that only one at a time goes to the wicket. The field is disposed as in the diagram, each with a "Spoonbill." The skill of the striker is (the balls (2) being first placed at equal distance in front of the wicket), to place them, being first struck in rapid succession through the half-rings, poles or field. Upon the success of this depends the numbers scored. The dexterity required to place the balls, with a good field, is not so easy to acquire as one would imagine.

The efforts of the fielders in return, each in his or her appointed place, as in the cricket field, and with their "spoonbill" is to check, not strike, the balls, the rights of the one last touching (provided the rules are adhered to) extending to putting the striker out, if he or she can, by throwing through the wicket. The striker can be put out in other ways by a catch or "fouls."

This Inter-Colonial cricket match between Sydney and Melbourne was played in the 1870's on the Cricket Association Ground, Moore Park, showing how Sydney was at last caching up with Melbourne in the scope of amenities for the game. Even top hatted Gentlemen were attracted to the game.

With the two balls so quickly following each other in the field, there is often some sharp work to prevent scoring, and active defence is required. The balls are similar to those used in lawn tennis, but are knitted to bring up to the required size. The game, notwithstanding the unusual bustle involved may be, as to the scoring, understood in a few moments by any onlooker.

Of course, it is governed by a number of carefully prepared rules. Mr Ironside has been negotiating with the Messrs. Cohen and Co, of George Street, about the materials, and it is not improbable they will be appointed sole agents for all in connection with the game.

Enough is enough. I will end the description of the game there before total exhaustion takes place, and will omit the very complicated diagram of the field. Little wonder that the game of Frisquet never got off the ground in Sydney or elsewhere.

But women on the cricket fields of the world were not to be denied and in time they organised their own games, and even test matches between competing countries. And to make up time for arriving late on the scene the Aussie girls eventually became the world champions of the sport.

And finally it should be remembered that they also added to the lexicon of the sport by adding a new term to cricket. This came to public light in 1980 when an English women's cricket team came to Australia to do battle with the locals. At a press conference a male reporter rather cheekily asked the Captain of the English team, Rachel Hahoe-Flynt, whether women cricketers used the same protectors as their male counterparts.

The Captain dealt with the question thus: "Yes, we do, but ours are slightly different and we don't call them boxes. We call them man-hole covers."

MENTOR AND MANAGER

John Conway was only four years older than Dave Gregory but he had a lot of experience of the team side of cricket and became a mentor to Gregory and his very capable Manager of the team that Gregory took to England in 1878.

J. CONWAY.

E. GREGORY.

Dave Gregory was one of the real movers and shakers in the latter half of the 19th Century, being Captain of the combined Australian team in the first Test Matches, and the organising Captain of the first white all professional team to England in 1878. He came from a great cricketing family and was a no hold bards sort of player and captain.

CHAPTER 12

The Dave Gregory Tour

After the win in the first test match against the Lillywhite team in Melbourne it was inevitable that there should result in a lot of speculation in cricket circles about the possibility of a tour of white Australians to England, though some critics considered the idea premature and presumptuous. "One butterfly doesn't make a summer" was a common comment at the time.

However, a lot of the key players were quite keen on the idea, and leading this group was Dave Gregory, Captain of the New South Wales team and also Captain of the winning Australian side in the first test.

Dave Gregory came from the famous Gregory family who have an almost continuous record in Australian cricket for more than a hundred years with members having played in eighty six test matches against England.

The sire of this unusual and remarkable cricket family was Edward William Gregory who came to New South Wales from England in 1813, and who played in club cricket in the Sydney area from 1826 onward. He had seven sons, five of whom played for New South Wales in inter-colonial matches between 1861 and 1884. Two of his sons played in the first test match against England in 1877. A grandson Sydney Edward Gregory (1870-1929) went to England in the test team of 1890 and made sixteen subsequent tours of England, the last time in 1912 as Captain. In all he played in 52 tests against England. One of Sydney's brothers, Charles W.Gregory (1878-1910) in a match against Queensland in the 1906-7 season made a score of 383, then an Australian record.

With this sort of family background, Dave Gregory was a very significant figure in Australian cricket history in the 1870's, so it was not surprising that his advocacy of a tour of Britain struck a chord with a veteran of an earlier age, John Conway, who was born in 1842, and was a great all-rounder. He captained the South Melbourne Club cricket team for many years and in 1862 played against Stevenson's first touring team.

He was an adviser to James Lillywhite's team, and he strongly supported Dave Gregory in his campaign for a team to tour England, eventually becoming team manager when it came to fruition.

But Gregory and his supporters had to overcome enormous obstacles before this could come about. And the biggest obstacle in their way was the long standing and never ending rivalry between Melbourne and Sydney. It seems the two cities could never agree on anything, They both baulked at the idea of sending an Australian team sponsored and financed jointly by the two cities. And both Sydney and Melbourne were not keen on taking individual responsibility because the team would have to contain a mix of players from both states.

It became clear to Gregory and his supporters that they could get no support from the two Sydney and Melbourne authorities. And they were knocked back went they asked major companies in both cities to sponsor them. In the end they decided they would have to finance the whole venture themselves, a very risky undertaking.

Gregory broke the news to his players saying they would each have to put up fifty pounds to cover their shipping costs over to England. And they had be prepared to undertake a number of benefit games in New South Wales, Queensland, Victoria and New Zealand to raise funds for extra expenses involved. To handle this Gregory formed a private company with the promise of dividends to the team if the tour produced a profit.

The team assembled in Sydney on November 3, 1877 and immediately set about making their fund raising tour. With funds in hand from the tour they embarked on the City of Sydney, from Sydney, on March 29, 1878 arriving at Liverpool on May 13.

The first white Australian tour was about to begin and the team comprised: John Conway (Manager), Dave Gregory (Captain), F.R. Spofforth, F.E. Allan, G.H. Bailley, T. Horan, T.W. Garrett, A.C. Bannerman, C. Bannerman, H.F. Boyle, W.L. Murdoch and M. Blackham. With William Midwinter, who had gone on ahead to join them in England.

CHAPTER 13

Off to a Bad Start

The first match of the Gregory tour was played at Nottingham on the Trent Bridge ground on May 20, 21 and 22, only a few days after the team had arrived in England and before they had time to get their land legs and to come to terms with the bleak light. It was staged before big crowds estimated at between 7000 and 8000, and it was no help to the visitors that the weather the previous days had soaked the pitch into an extremely dead one.

In a nutshell the match was a disaster for the Australians who scored only 63 in the first innings and 76 in the second, against Notts single innings of 153. The only batsman to display any form was Garrett (with 20 and 21) and Midwinter, who had joined the team when it first arrived, who scored 13 in the first innings and another 13 not out in the second.

The loss of their first match by an innings and 14 runs had the cricket writers of the English press chortling with glee and predicting that the Australian team would prove to be a walkover for the powerful teams it would be meeting during this tour.

As a result of the poor press they had received from the Nottis game only a small crowd turned up on the first day of the second game against a very strong MCC All England side which included their old adversary Dr Grace. And their chances were further dimmed by the fact that heavy rain had turned both the wicket and the outfield into a quagmire. It was clear to everybody that this wasn't going to be a high scoring game as all the odds favoured the bowlers.

The match started on May 27 at The Oval and was scheduled for three days, but was all over in one, with the visitors slaying the mighty dragon as a result of an inspired burst of brilliant bowling by Spofforth, Allan and Boyle which shattered the greatly favoured English team which could only muster 33 runs in the first innings and 19 in the second. The great Dr Grace went for a meager four runs in the first innings and was bowled

Before

and After

*Before the match one of the leading cartoonists featured the top sketch showing a healthy old
British Lion feeding gruel to a very seedy Kangaroo. After the match he had to do a backflip. Now
the strong Kangaroo is administering the gruel to a very sickly old Lion.*

by Spofforth for a duck in the second.

The Australians scored only 41 runs in the first innings, with Midwinter top scoring with 10 runs, and only needed 12 runs to win in the second a score that was achieved with the loss of only one wicket.

Spofforth took the bowling honours for the visitors with 10 wickets in the match (6 in the first innings and 6 in the second) for a total of 20 runs. Boyle took three wickets in the first innings and six in the second for 19 runs.

The unexpected Australian victory at Lords caused the English cricket writers to do a detailed analysis of the Australian team for the first time. They observed that every one of the Australians was a superb fielder, and they expressed wonder at the unorthodox bowling of Spofforth, a very tall thin man who bowled his medium pacers down from a great height with deadly aim, often mixing them with slow deliveries which invariably bamboozled the batsman.

Even the non-cricketing journals joined in the fun and Vanity Fair named Spofforth as the "Demon Bowler" – a nickname that was to stick with him for the rest of his career.

The cartoonists of the period had a field day depicting the spindly figure of Spofforth, while one paper which had depicted the Australians as a weakly Kangaroo being fed gruel by the mighty English Lion before the match, had to change its tune and in a revised cartoon after the Lords match they had the now healthy Kangaroo feeding gruel to a sickly Old Lion.

All this valuable and unexpected publicity resulted in record crowds flocking to following matches causing the Aussies to really laugh all the way to the bank. In real fiscal terms the big crowds meant that the financial success of the tour was now assured.

Three British artists Showing how they Saw Spofforth

Australia against The Marylebone Cricket Club at Lords 1878.

An artist from the English magazine, The Illustrated Sporting and Dramatic News was at this Australia v England match at the Oval in 1878 and caught Spofforth ready to bowl to Dr Grace, the unusual delivery about to take flight.

CHAPTER 14

The Triumphal Tour

With the unexpected victory at Lords behind them, the Australian team set off on what was to be a triumphal tour from one end of England to the other, their next target being the mighty Yorkshire, played at Huddersfield on May 30 & 31.

Yorkshire scored 72 and 73 in their two innings, while Australia was well in front with scores of 110 and 78, winning by six wickets. Spofforth was again the star bowler taking five wickets in each innings.

The Australians then tackled a strong team from Surrey, again having a clear cut win over the locals. Surrey scored 107 and 80 in their two innings while the Australians scored 110 and 78 for five wickets, winning by a clear six wickets. Spofforth was again the destroyer of Surrey taking eight wickets in the first innings and three in the second innings. An interesting sidelight to this match was that the Surrey wicketkeeper was Edward Pooley, who starred in the Christchurch, New Zealand, incident of James Lillywhite's 1876 test match tour of Australia and New Zealand.

Against the Australian eleven for Surrey Pooley scored a handy 29 in the first innings and as wicketkeeper stumped both Horan and Spofforth and caught A Bannerman, obviously having fully recovered from the injuries he suffered at the hands of his vocal and dangerous betting adversary in Christchurch.

The Australians then moved on to Elland where they played a local team against the odds of 18 again wining comfortably with innings of 99 and 83 against the locals of 29 and 66. Spofforth was again the main destroyer with five wickets in the first innings and ten in the second.

Moving on to Batley on June 10 the Australians tackled a local team, again against the odds of 18, and struck constant rain which washed out two days of play. This game was drawn after the Australians had scored 160 and the Batley 18 had scored 59 for 10 wickets.

A few days later at Longsight the Australians again struck bad weather when they played a local team against the odds of 18 which included G .F.Grace, brother of the great Dr Grace. The Australians could only score 67 in both innings, while the Longsighters managed 63 and 67 to win the match by two wickets – their first defeat since their opening match at Notts.

Two days later, on Monday June 17, the Australians were called on to play one of the most memorable and unusual matches of the tour, against The Gentlemen of England. Not a Professional in sight. The match was played at The Oval and the Gentlemen's side included Dr Grace and his brother and Gilbert, Steel and Lucas. An estimated seven to eight thousand spectators attended each day despite the extra sixpence charged over the usual entry fee of one shilling. The weather was bad, causing long delays, and the pitch was very heavy. The Australian team made only 75 and 63 in their two innings and were outclassed by the Gentlemen who scored 139 and thus had an easy win by an innings and one run.

Two losses in a row were quite a blow for the Australians and it took a lot of wind out of their sails, but they made up for it later in the week when they played and defeated a strong Middlesex side at Lords before a crowd of 5000 spectators.

On this occasion the weather was fine and the wicket, though a little soft, was far more playable than the pitches played on in the previous weeks, resulting in some very good scores to the great delight of the crowd. But before play began a tense scene was played out when the formidable Dr. Grace, who was not playing in the match, appeared and confronted Midwinter, who had played in most of the matches up to that date, declaring that his contract with Gloucestershire prohibited him from playing with any other team. Midwinter, who up to that time had proven to be one of the star all rounders of the Australian team, had to fall into line and he did not take part in any further games for the touring side.

Very harsh words were exchanged between Dr Grace and Gregory and the tour manager, John Conway. Grace later apologised to Gregory, but refused to apologise to Conway and feelings between Grace and the whole team remained tense for the rest of the tour.

The Australian team made 165 in their first innings and 240 in the second. Middlesex only managed 122 and 185. For once Spofforth's skills failed him as he did not take a wicket in either innings. But he made up for his bowling lapse by making top score for the innings of 56 runs.

After this triumph the Australian team moved on to Birmingham where they played a district side against the odds of 22 players. Australia made a modest 105 and were 116 for six wickets when the match was drawn on the second day, Birmingham having the advantage with a score of 123. However Spofforth had recovered from his bowling lapse at Lords as he took eleven wickets in 40 overs for 60 runs.

The next match of the tour was at Hunslet where the Australians played a district team against the odds of 18 players, and again had a drawn game. The Australians scored 205 and 180 while Hunslet were 228 and nine wickets down in their second innings for 28 runs when play was abandoned. Spofforth again dominated the bowling with eight wickets in the first Hunslet inning and three in the second innings.

The Australians then returned to Yorkshire for a return match at Sheffield starting on July 1 and on this occasion they lost to the home side. The Australians batted first and made only miserly scores of 88 and 104 which the home side were able to top easily with scores of 167 and one wicket for 26, winning by nine wickets.

The Australians made up for this a few days later when they had a substantial victory over a Stockport and District team, scoring 163 and 225 against the home side's 105 and 134, winning by a margin of 149 runs.

The Australians followed this match with one against C.J. Thornton's Eleven on the Orleans Club grounds at Twickenham, the ground for the first time being thrown open to the public. This was the elite of English cricket and present were Lord Londondesborough, Earl Sefton, the Duke of Beaufort and many minor celebrities.

The Australians won the toss and got off to a good start when the opener A Bannerman made 71 of a total of 171. They followed up with 172 in their second innings. Mr Thornton's eleven responded with 132 and 137 with two wickets down, so the match was drawn.

Australia found itself again playing amongst the nobs of English cricket a few days later when it faced the Gentlemen of Wales at Swansea, a match played against the odds of 18 players. The Australians made 219 runs and then bowled out the Gentlemen of Wales twice for 94 and 84, winning by 37 runs. The destroyer again was Spofforth who took ten wickets in the first innings and a further six wickets in the second innings.

A follow up match of Werneth and Oldham players against the odds of 18 was played at Oldham before a crowd estimated at between 8000 and 9000. The locals batted first and made 138 and 117, while the Australians responded with 123 and 112 for seven wickets when play was abandoned with a draw.Spofforth again was the main bowler for the Australians taking six wickets in the first innings and eight in the second.

The Australians then tackled a Leicestershire side at the County Club, Leicester, with the home side winning the toss and batting, and the two openers Wheeler and Sankey chalked up impressive totals of 60 and 79 respectively. Wheeler followed up with 65 in the second inning. The first inning total of 193 was followed by Australia with 130. Leicestershire then made the mistake of declaring at 129 for four wickets in the second innings whereupon Australia responded with a second innings total of 210 for two wickets, thus winning by eight wickets. The top scorer was C. Bannerman with a run out 133, the first century of the tour.

Their next match was played on July 18, 19 and 20, against The Hull Town Club, on a small ground which was ideal for good scores. The Hull side batted first and made an impressive 250 but collapsed in the second innings with only 68 runs scored. Australia responded with a massive 305 in the first innings and 15 in the second without loss to comfortably win the match. Top scorers for Australia were Allan 78, Blackham 63 and Horan 60. Of the bowlers Boyle was the chief destroyer with three wickets in the first innings and eight in the second.

On July 22 the Australians moved on to Lords ground where they played a Cambridge University team at its full strength. Cambridge batted first and made an impressive 286 which proved enough to win the match as the Australians could only muster 111 and 102 thus losing out to the University team by an innings and 72 runs. Quite a drubbing.

On July 25, 26 and 27 they made up for this when they played a 22 side of Crewe and District in wet weather. The Australians chalked up innings of 130 and 102 which was sufficient to outplay the lengthy Crew side which managed only 64 and 79. Again Spofforth was the destroyer taking ten wickets in both innings.

On July 29, 30 and 31 the team moved on to Keighley where they played a district team against the odds of 18 where they won by seven wickets with scores of 206 and 32 and the Keighley side of 102 and 133 Spofforth again scored an even ten wickets in the first innings and a fairly miserly two in the second innings.

On August 1 they moved to Rochdale to play against the odds of 18 and had a drawn match when they scored 159 and 72 against Rochdale who completed only one innings of 124.

Another match against the odds of 22 was played on August 5 and 6, at Buxton against a Buxton District team which scored a fairly miserly 77 runs with twelve wickets falling to Spofforth. Australia responded with 97. In their second innings the home team scored 124 and at close of play the Australians had lost one wicket for 17 when play was abandoned and the match was drawn.

A one day match was hastily arranged for the following day, August 7, at nearby Burnley against the odds of 18. The Burnley side batted first and made a poor start, losing ten wickets for only 20 runs due to the efforts of Spofforth and Boyle, but they recovered to make 102 runs .The Australians did not do much better making only 47 for eight wickets before rain caused play to be abandoned and the match declared a draw.

The Australians were now playing most days of the week, which must have put an enormous strain on them. On August 8, the day after the scratch one day game at Burnley, they were called on to play a match against the odds of 18 against the Stanley Club at Stanley Park, Liverpool. The Australians batted first and made a respectable 238 thanks to the efforts of Gregory 70 and Blackham 58. The Stanley Club 18 could only respond with efforts of 71 and 91, again thanks to Spofforth who took ten wickets in the first innings and nine in the second.

As the match had been finished in two days of the three allocated, on the third day (August 9) they played a scratch one day match when the Stanley Club made quite a respectable 193. But time had run out and the Australians were 26 with two wickets down when play had to be abandoned.

On August 12 the Australians went on to play a Dudley & District team against the odds of 18. As the wicket was dead the Dudley team sent the Australians in to bat which proved to be a wise move as the visitors could make only 59 runs. But the home team did no better and responded with a miserable 33. This time Boyle did all the damage with twelve wickets. (Spofforth did not play in this match). The Australians made a much better total of 233, while Dudley could only respond with another miserable 40 for seven wickets down in their second innings thus managing a draw.

The Australians then moved on to Lancashire where they played a county team at Old Trafford Ground on a wicket very heavy from recent rains. The locals made 97 and 162 to which the Australians responded with 140 and 47 for the loss of no wickets. Match drawn.

The Australians then moved on to Yeadon & District playing against the odds of 18 with two of their best players missing, Charles Bannerman ill and Gregory away on leave. The Australians won the toss and sent the locals in to bat, dismissing them for 97 with Spofforth again being deadly taking nine wickets. They did no better in their second innings with 71, but this was enough to beat the Aussies who managed only 54 and 84 in their two innings.

On August 24 the Australians went to Scarborough to play a district team against the odds of 18. The visitors batted first and came up with a respectable first innings score of 295, Spofforth being top scorer with 64 and Blackham run out for 56. The home side managed only 124 and 125 in their two innings, leaving the Australians winners by an innings and 46 runs.

On August 26 the visitors moved down to Hastings to play a district team against the odds of 18. The local team could only muster 131 and 82, which the Australians easily capped with their single innings of 260, thanks to a fine century of 106 by Bailey – the second century scored by an Australian on the tour. Murdoch weighed in with a handy 78, giving the visitors an easy victory by an innings and 47 runs.

The Australians then played a tight game against a county team of Sussex, scoring 75 and 63 in their two innings, against the home side scores of 80 and 47. With time to spare they then played an impromptu game against the Gentlemen of Sussex who scored 128 runs. The Australians responded with 91 for the loss of three wickets. Match drawn.

The next match, played on September 2 at the Oval was the cause of much dissension in the English cricket world. The Surrey County Club had granted use of the Oval free of charge to the visitors in the belief that they would be playing against a strong team of leading Professionals. But top Professionals were thin on the ground and a crowd of 10,000 believed they had been cheated. Lillywhite was captain of the Eleven Players and because the ground was so soft from recent rains he sent the Australians in to bat, a fairly wise move as they scored only 77 runs in their first innings and 89 in their second. Charles Bannerman was the only one to make a score in the first innings, finishing with 51 of the 77 runs scored. The English team did little better scoring only 82 and 76 thus giving the visitors a win by eight runs.

The next match, against Gloucestershire on September 5 and 6 on the Clifton College Grounds, saw the Australians putting up a much better show winning with ease, with 10 wickets in hand. The Australians scored 183 (of which Spofforth was top scorer with 44 and 17 without loss, to the home team's 112 and 83, Spofforth taking seven wickets in their first innings and five in the second.

On September 7, while still in Gloucestershire, the Australians played a Gentlemen of England side, again on the Clifton Ground. The visitors compiled 157 and a hefty 249 in the second innings. C. Bannerman scored 21 in the first innings and 54 in the second, while the wicketkeeper Murdoch was not out 44 in the first innings and scored 49 in the second. The Gentleman managed only 109 in their innings and the match was drawn.

The Australians played their last match in the London area on September 9 and 10 at Princes against Players with rain interrupting play for long periods on both days. Australia made a very respectable 236 with Dave Gregory top scoring with 67 and C. Bannerman contributing 61. Players responded with 160 and the match was drawn.

The fairly battle wearied Australians then took the overnight train to Glasgow to play out their final two matches of the series in Scotland.

The first of these matches, against twelve of the West of Scotland Club resulted in an easy win for the visitors who scored 268, of which Murdoch contributed 87, Spofforth 48 and Gregory 41. West of Scotland could only muster 99 and 85 in their two innings, Garrett took six wickets in the first innings and Spofforth eight wickets in the second.

The final match of the tour against the odds of 18 Sunderland players took place on Septmeber 16 with Spofforth, Horan and Bailey absent, their places being taken by Australians then living in England. And the Australians went down in this last match by 71 runs, scoring just 77 and 58 in their two innings, against the 59 and 147 notched up by the home side. Garrett was the star bowler taking ten wickets in the first innings while Allan took eight wickets in the second innings.

CHAPTER 15

Tour Summary

In what must have been an extremely exhausting tour the Australians played 41 matches in England and Scotland, winning 19, losing seven and with fifteen drawn , mainly due to being washed out by rain in what was an unusually wet English summer.

Most of the matches were relatively low scoring games due to the sodden pitches which made batting difficult. As a result only two centuries were scored in the tour one against even sides of eleven and one in the against the odds matches. Charles Bannerman, the star Australian player, was slow to get started on the wet pitches but once he found touch he was well up to his near best form and was rated by English cricket writers as being amongst the best players of his time. But bowler Spofforth and witckkeepers Blackham and Murdoch showed unusual skills with both bat and ball right through the tour.

Spofforth, who quickly earned the title of The Dmon Bowler, lived up to his name as the top wicket taker of the tour bowling 753 overs, of which an incredible 274 were maidens, and taking 107 wickets for an average 64. He was a long way ahead of the second best wicket taker, Boyle, who bowled 440 overs, of which 194 were maidens, for 64 wicket for 626 runs. Allan who was rated top bowler of the team back in Australia, struggled to get wickets with his 377 overs (179 of which were maidens) for just 26 wickets for 605 runs. Garrett with 301 overs (147 maidens) took 38 wickets for 147 runs, a very economical 10 runs a wicket. These figures were only for the most important eleven a side matches. No records appear to have been kept for the matches Australia played against the odds of 18 and sometimes 22 players, otherwise Spofforth's big haul of wickets in these matches would have shot through the ceiling.

It was Spofforth who attracted the most press coverage during the tour with his unusual delivery. The anonymous cricket writer of the London Daily News summed him up thus:

"Mr Spofforth has earned for himself the highest bowling renown. Not even George Freeman of Tarrant, at his best, ever created such panic among batsmen. Taking a long run, delivering the ball at the full extent of an unusually large reach, and so disguising his intentions that few can tell whether the coming ball will be one of the famous 'Yorkers' or a slow breakback. Mr Spofforth is simply the most puzzling and destructive bowler this generation has seen".

On the batting side Charles Bannerman stood out in both the main eleven aside matches and those played against the odds. In the main games he played in 17 matches and scored 720 runs with a top score of 133. In the games against the odds he scored 513 runs in his 16 innings with a top score of 54.

His nearest rival was Tom Horan who in the main matches scored 376 runs with a top score of 64. In the Odds matches he made 439 runs with a top score of 70. Their nearest rival in the batting order was bowler Spofforth who scored 335 in the main matches and 358 in the Odds games, his top scores being 56 and 64 respectively, indicating what a key player he was to the side.

The cricket writers were also much taken with the way the two Australian wicketkeepers, Blackham and Murdoch, stood up to the wickets, even against the fastest bowlers, easily taking the ball on both leg and off stumps with the same apparent ease.

And the cricket writers were also full of praise for the high standard of all the Australians in the field, noting this was very rare among English cricket teams of the period. And Dave Gregory's captaincy skills came in for a lot of praise as the writers were quick to notice the way he used his brain to sum up each new batsman at the crease, quickly changing his bowlers around to exploit possible weaknesses in the newcomers.

And, above all, the critics were loud in their praise of the sportsmanship of the Australian team. Not a whisper of the sledging of present day times which has become such a disgrace for Australian teams.

One aspect of the tour which set ablaze a controversy amongst the English Professionals – the Players – and that was the fact that the tour had been a huge financial success for the Australians. Their initial fifty pound contributions had earned them each a dividend of seven hundred and fifty pounds, a very healthy sum in those far off days when wages were around a pound a week.

Perhaps out of jealously the Professionals launched a campaign against James Lillywhite, who had led the previous English tour of Australia. The Professionals who had been paid a meagre five pounds each per match, alleged that from a final testimonial match of the tour Lillywhite had paid the Australian team members each twenty pounds, a total of two hundred and twenty pounds. Lillywhite heatedly rejected the claims. He admitted a payment of two hundred and twenty pounds had been made but he said this was for general expenses in staging the game. The Professionals tried to draw the Australian touring side into the controversy on the grounds that most of them must have been recipients of this bonus, but the team clammed up and maintained their silence, while the controversy raged in the English press.

And the Australian team took their farewell from Liverpool on the City of Richmond for America, on September 22 without making any admissions on the Lillywhite matter. A crowd estimated at 2000 was on the docks to farewell them as they set sail for New York, where further cricketing adventures awaited them.

Fred Spofforth by general acclaim had to be the Winner of the Best Player of the Tour award for his huge haul of wickets in almost every game of wickets in almost every game he played in.

CHAPTER 16

Australia v New York

When it comes to naming famous cricket cities these days New York does mot spring to mind, but things were quite different back in 1898 when Dave Gregory's famous cricket team was travelling the world. At that time New York had a large population of English cricket fanatics determined to keep up the traditions of the Old Country come what may.

So, when Gregory's team reached New York after their very successful tour of the British Isles they were greeted on the docks by Mr Green, the Vice President of the New York Cricket Club, and other executives, and by their own team manager John Conway who had travelled on ahead of the team to arrange a series of matches in America.

Their first match was against the odds of 18 drawn from various clubs around New York by the St George's Club, and was played on the club's Holboken ground which had been specially prepared and was in fine condition. The weather was perfect for the match played over two days, October 1 and 2, and a good crowd estimated at 3000 turned up to see the match.

Gregory sent the New Yorkers in to bat and such was the effectiveness of the bowling of Spofforth and Garrett that they soon had the locals dismissed for a very modest 63 runs.

The Australians then went into bat, confident they could easily beat this target, but immediately they ran into an unexpected hurdle in the shape of an ace which the New Yorkers had kept up their sleeve. This took the form of a former baseball pitcher named J.E. Sprague, whose very accurate under arm deliveries were so precise that the two seasoned Bannerman brothers who opened were totally at loss of how to handle this unexpected assault. The match ground to a sudden halt as Sprague delivered up fourteen maiden overs in a row, and the two Bannerman brothers were dismissed for a miserly three (for Charles) and one for his brother. The rest of the team did not fare much better and finished up

T. GARRETT.

J. BLACKHAM.

G. H. BAILEY.

C. BANNERMAN

D. W. GREGORY.

W. MURDOCK.

A. BANNERMAN.

*Harper's Magazine in its
October 19, 1878 issue had
its artist do sketches of the
Australian cricket team
visiting New York.*

H. BOYLE.

F. ALLAN.

T. HORAN.

F. SPOFFORTH.

with a first innings total of 70.

In their second innings the New Yorkers managed a score of 98 and the Australians managed to get the necessary 92 runs for five wickets, to claim a victory. But it had been a fairly close and unexpected shave for the visitors.

For the bowlers Spofforth was the star getting eight wickets in the first New Yorker innings and a handy haul of eleven in the second innings.

Somewhat chastened by this experience they went on to Philadelphia the next day, October 3, where they played an even elevens match against a much younger and more experienced team who scored an impressive 196 runs in their first innings.

The Australians got a shock when their star batsman Charles Bannerman was out for a duck in the first over. A bit later Gregory met the same fate when his wicket was shattered by a fast ball that got through his usually solid defences. The middle order rallied and managed to carry the total through to 150 just before close of play on the first day.

News of a close match spread and the second day saw a record crowd estimated at 10,000 line up for the conclusion. Half way through the second innings of the home team there was an unusual upset when the score was 19 for four wickets down. The star batsman of the home team, Dan Newhall, when playing forward to a ball from Allan, the ball went into the hands of Blackhan who raised the bails just as Dan put the bat down. The umpire declared not out, but Blackham heatedly disputed this and when the umpire would not yield, the Australian team walked off the field. After an hour's parleying the team agreed to resume and finish the match, and the home side finished with a score of 53 in their second innings. This left the Australians needing 100 runs to win. They had scored 56 for the loss of four wickets when the light gave out and the match finished with a draw.

The Australians then crossed the border and played two matches in Canada. The Australians had an easy win against the odds of 18 at Toronto on October 8 and had another easy win at Montreal on October 10 and 11 against a side of 22. It appears that cricket was by no means as popular in the cold of Canada as in sunnier New York and Philadelphia.

The Australians then recrossed the border into the United States and played a match at Detroit on October 15 and 16 against the odds of 18, the Peninsula Club of Detroit. Again the visitors had an easy victory.

They then moved on to California where they played a three day match against the odds of 22, playing the Pacific Slope Club of San Francisco beginning on October 26. The match was played at the Recreation Grounds and attracted a small but high class crowd which included the Mayor of San Francisco, a bevy of officials from the British Embassy and several millionaires. Most of the socialities of the city were present and it soon became a social event rather than a cricket match.

The Australians batted first and had no trouble amassing 302 runs, with Charles Bannerman being the main scorer with 78. The Californians could only muster 63 and 105 in their two innings, thus giving the visitors a very comprehensive victory of an innings and 124 runs. For once Spofforth wasn't the main destroyer, although he took seven wickets in the first innings and only a solitary one in the second. All the laurels for the match went to Boyle who snared a remarkable 15 wickets in the second innings, while Allan took honours in the first innings with 12 wickets.

After the match there was a substantial farewell banquet to the Aussies who were soon to depart for home after a magnificent tour of England, Wales, Scotland, Canada and the United States.

On their arrival in Sydney in November they were greeted on the docks by thousands of cheering fans.

But there was to be little rest for the returning heroes as in the following month, December of 1878, there arrived from England a team led by Lord Harris aiming to play Australia in two test matches. This tour was to turn out to be the most controversial of all the visiting teams , at least until the event of the Bodyline series in the next century.

CHAPTER 17

The Great Lord Harris Cometh

Over in England Lords are pretty plentiful and usually are treated with great respect, but in far off Australia they are a pretty rare species and the locals are hard put to know how to treat them. If they get the impression they are a bit Up Themselves they are likely to get the Tall Poppy treatment which tends to bring them down to earth a bit.

And this is what happened to Lord Harris when he brought a team to Australia in 1878-9, a team that arrived hard on the heels of the returning Gregory team visit to England.

With Lord Harris as Captain, the team comprised A.N. Hornby, C.A. Absalom, A.J. Webb, K. Hone, H.C. Maul, F.A. MacKinnon, V. Boyle and L.S. Schulz, all Gentleman players and two Professionals Emmett and Ulyett, who Lord Harris had been reluctantly forced to include because he could not round up a full team of Gentlemen.

The team left Southhampton on October 17, 1878 and reached Adelaide early in December where they had a game against an Adelaide team of 16 players.

They then moved to Melbourne to play in the first test match on the Melbourne Cricket Ground on January 2, 3 and 4. Lord Harris had a strong batting team so decided to bat when he won the toss on the first morning despite the fact that the match was delayed by a heavy storm. His team quickly fell to the wiles of Spofforth who got the first Hat Trick in test cricket. England were all out for 113 and the Australian side responded with a brisk 256, of which A.C. Bannerman, Charles Bannerman's younger brother, was playing in his first test. England made 160 in the second inning, giving Australia a victory of ten wickets after they scored the necessary 19 runs without loss of a wicket.

After sundry state and district matches Lord Harris brought his team to Sydney where they were scheduled to play the second test match – a game that never took place as a result of a great upset to an earlier game against a New South Wales side which was badly disrupted when the crowd stormed the pitch on the second day, Saturday, February 8, 1879, a day of shame for cricket generally and which severely strained relations with Britain for several years.

Lord Harris got his team off to a flying start with an opening partnership of Hornby and Lucas of 125 runs, finishing the innings with a respectable 267. In reply New South Wales were all out for 177, Murdoch having batted right through the innings for 82 not out.

The home team had to follow on and when the score was 18 Murdoch was given out in very controversial circumstances by George Coulthard, a Victorian player employed Lord Harris as their umpire. The idea of neutral umpires at both ends was still a way off and the old practice of each team appointing an umpire was till in force.

On the previous day Coulthard had made another bad decision declaring Lord Harris not out to a catch from a nick that could be heard all over the ground.

Murdoch believed he was not out, but walked any way. The crowd however, didn't take kindly to Coulthard's decision and commenced very loud booing, and uproar broke out, fuelled by a group of Melbourne bookmakers who had heavily bet on a win by New South Wales.

In a coverage of the incident in his book SPORTS, Keith Dunstan put up the interesting, but quite logical, theory that the crowd was not so much against the Englishmen, but were against Coulthard because he came from Victoria and was a prominent member of the Victorian Establishment.

At that time the Melbourne Establishment dominated the game in Australia and the intense rivalry between the two cities resulted in the crowd being more suspicious of a Victorian umpire than an English one. It should be remembered that the victim Murdoch was a very prominent and popular Sydney player.

When no batsman came out to replace Murdoch, Lord Harris left the field to find out the cause of the delay. He was met by the New South Wales Captain, Dave Gregory, who informed him that he was lodging a complaint against Coulthard's umpiring, and he resisted all attempts by

Lord Harris to change his mind.

While this discussion was taking place an unnamed member of the English team allegedly shouted to the crowd, "You are nothing but sons of convicts." Lord Harris and his players later denied this was said, but the Sydney Morning Herald tracked down several well known members of the crowd who insisted the words had been used.

This comment caused a huge upheaval amongst the crowd of spectators who surged on to the field and began to harass the English team and Coulthard, In the pavilion Lord Harris noticed this and hurried back on to the field, making his way fairly roughly to where Coulthard stood and was being abused. A team member, A.M. Hornby seized the main demonstrator, a small man, and forcibly removed him from the ground and had him locked up in the Common Room.

By this time the number of intruders on the field was estimated at a thousand. Punches were thrown on both sides and insults filled the air. It took the small force of police present quite a while to clear the ground of intruders, by which time Lord Harris was back in the pavilion trying to persuade the stubborn Dave Gregory to change his mind. But Gregory still refused.

But then a piece of Australian history was introduced into the impasse as Lord Harris approached the other umpire, who happened to be Edmund Barton, who later became Premier of New South Wales, when he acquired the nickname of "Tosspot Toby" as a result of his drinking problem. And later still he became the first Prime Minister of Australia with the coming of Federation in 1901.

Barton supported the decision made by his fellow umpire, and when Harris asked him whether under any of the laws of cricket he could claim the game, Barton replied: "I'll give it to you in two minutes if the New South Welshmen don't return." This really pulled the rug from under Gregory, since he had appointed Barton as his team's umpire. When Lord Harris confronted him with Barton's ultimatum, Gregory was forced to reluctantly resume the match.

However, when the replacement batsman for Murdoch took to the field, the crowd saw that Coulthard was still the umpire and they started to invade the ground again. Twice the police cleared the ground of spectators, and twice they came back in large numbers. They made it plain that there was no way they would let the game proceed with Coulthard as umpire. At 6pm play was abandoned for day with Lord Harris and a few of his men standing firm in case the match was given against them if they left the field.

There was no play the next day, Sunday, but when play resumed on the Monday there were only about fifteen hundred spectators present and they sat grimly silent in their seats while the farce was played out, Australia being dismissed for 49 runs and the match was awarded to England.

The consequences of the incident were massive and widespread. The Sydney newspapers and journals, while describing the whole incident as disgraceful, did back up their team on the matter of Coulthard's alleged impartiality. On the other hand the Melbourne based Australian commented that Sydney was becoming notorious for that sort of rowdyism, and claimed that Melbourne players in Inter-Continental matches frequently went there in fear of their lives.

Lord Harris added fuel to the fires when he wrote a long letter home giving his version of events. This letter was printed in the English papers and promptly reprinted back in the Australian press only too willing to keep the pot boiling.

The Illustrated Sydney News led the pack condemning Lord Harris, in the February 1879 issue running a cartoon showing an Australian Squatter wielding a big whip and thrashing Lord Harris, depicted as a sheep fleeing from the scene. And to add further insult it published the following poem:

Sing we of Lordy Harris
Scion of a noble race
Sick of London, Brighton, Paris
And every other place.
Swore by the crest deep craven
On family silver spoons
That he'ed ne'er be washed or shaven
Till he'd thrashed the parlous loons.

Came the morning of the struggle
Thrown aside were vest and coat,
And the "Fizz" went gurgle, gurgle
Down his Lordship's lordly throat

The members of the New South Wales Cricket Association did all they could to quell the spillover from the ugly events of the Saturday, and they apologised profusely to Lord Harris after the event. They also took action against a well known Victorian bookmaker and his cronies who appear to have started the trouble. They refunded them their entrance fees and then told them never to return to Sydney again.

They also pressed charges against two of the main participants in the rowdy demonstration on the field. Both men pleaded guilty to the charge of creating a public disorder, and expressed regret for their actions. They were fined forty shillings and ordered to pay another twenty one shillings professional costs, and five shillings for court costs.

But nothing could save the Lord Harris tour, and the second test scheduled for Sydney was cancelled. He was given a friendly farewell dinner in Melbourne, but Australia's sporting reputation had been severely damaged, and the next team to England got a very frosty welcome indeed.

Perhaps Lord Harris was a bit unlucky to have stirred up the Australian Tall Poppy syndrome, but he brought most of this on himself quite early in the tour as a result of him treating his two Professional players, Tom Emmett and George Ulyett, who were his main bowlers, quite differently from the rest of the Gentlemen players, very much in the style that Dr Grace had done on his Honeymoon tour.

It would seem that lords and cricket don't always mix successfully down under in the Antipodes.

THE DIPLOMATIC CAPTAIN

The leader of the 1879 ream to England was William (Billy) Murdoch, the NSW keeper and a much more temperate man than his predecessor Dave Gregory. He faced a very icy reception at first, but managed to win the Brits over from the anger they felt from the Sydney riots with Lord Harris's team.

FRIENDS!

LORD HARRIS A FRIEND!

The same cartoonist who did the Sketch of Murdoch above, also made the one on the left showing him shaking hands with Lord Harris. He titled his cartoon FRIENDS but was careful to add an exclamation mark to the word.

CHAPTER 18

The Birth Of The Ashes

The disastrous events of that day in February 1879 lingered on to haunt William Murdoch, the innocent fall guy who was given out on that fatal day, and who was the following year appointed Captain of the Australian side sent to England by the two main cricket associations in Sydney and Melbourne who had at last come to their senses on the need for join action in sponsoring touring teams.

If the Australians had thought that the storm of controversy had blown over in England in the ensuing year they were sadly mistaken. The reception the team received on its arrival in England was of glacial proportions, and everywhere they went they were snubbed, at least in the beginning of the tour.

The MCC made it plain that there would be no test matches that year and that they could not play on the MCC ground because it was fully booked. They received similar treatment from the counties, and were forced to advertise for games against the odds of 18 and 22.

Finally Dr Grace realised that the cold shoulder had been applied too heavily, and he came to the rescue by inviting them to play against his county side Gloucestershire, which was perhaps rubbing salt into old wounds as only two years previously Dave Gregory's team had boycotted the county because Dr Grace had forbidden Midwinter to play for the Australian team.

After that some of the other counties fell into line and suddenly found they could arrange some matches after all, and then, through the intervention of Dr Grace and Lord Harris, the MCC also did a back flip when it was persuaded to allow a game at The Oval, which became the first Test Match played in England.

Australia was without two of their star performers, Charles Bannerman, who was ill, and Spofforth who had broken a finger in a match at Scarborough. The English side was a reasonably good one, including Dr

Grace and with Lord Harris as Captain.

England made a great start with a first innings of 420 of which Grace scored 152. Australia replied with a fairly miserable total of 149 and the game looked to be all over. Australia had been forced to follow on, and here they rallied when their Captain Murdoch, who had made a duck in the first innings, responded with an unbeaten 153 in a total of 327. That left England with only 57 to make in its second innings to win, and without the magic of Spofforth the Australian side still faced defeat.

Lord Harris was so confident of victory that he changed the batting order and soon his side was in trouble with five wickets down for a modest 31. Then Dr Grace strode to the wicket and stemmed the tide for England to take a five wicket victory.

Although he was not aware of it at the time, Dr Grace had not only saved the day for England, but he had curiously saved the day for Australia as record crowds attended The Oval for the match, preventing it becoming a financial disaster for the Australians. And the crowds rallied around too with good attendances at all the remaining Australian matches.

And much of this success can be chalked up to the fact that Murdoch was a much more peaceful person than the rather pugnacious Gregory and he managed to restore harmony with the offended Englishmen.

In the 1881-2 season James Lillywhite, Alfred Shaw and Arthur Shrewbury organised a tour to Australia by a team of Professionals. Dr Grace of course was missing and the team was not a particularly strong one. Ironically it included William Midwinter, who thus gained the distinction of being the only person to play both for and against his original home country.

The English team played four test matches on this tour. The first was drawn and the second and third matches, both played in Sydney were won by Australia, while the fourth test was washed out by rain. There were no incidents in any of the games and the tour was a financial success. The old feuding was over and peace was restored at last on both sides of the world.

Following hard upon the heels of the fourth drawn test, an Australian team, again captained by Murdoch, left for another tour of England. Only one test match was scheduled and this had long been acclaimed as one of the greatest games ever played between the two countries, and it gave birth to the term Ashes.

On this tour Murdoch's team got off to a flying start with a nine wicket victory against Oxford University, thanks to a massive 206 runs notched up in three hours by a newcomer to the team, Bob Massie.

They then moved to Essex where Murdoch made 286 not out and Palmer took a hat trick, They scored a record 643 in their first and only innings eventually winning by 355 runs. They lost to Cambridge but then had a succession of second class wins before facing up at The Oval for the next test match. All the publicity for the pre-test wins ensured record crowds at Lords.

England fielded one of their strongest sides in years, its strength being gauged by the fact that Hornby, one of the best bats in England for many years batted at number ten in the first innings. Australia was handicapped by the fact that one of their leading bowlers, Palmer, could not play and had to be replaced by a nineteen year old novice, Sam Jones.

Murdoch won the toss and elected to bat but the team put up a very poor performance and were bundled out for a disastrous 63 runs. Playing conditions must have been poor that day because despite their huge batting line up, the English team made only a modest 101 in reply, thanks to some wonderful bowling by Spofforth.

Despite an opening partnership of 66 in the second innings, Australia failed to sparkle and were all out for 122, leaving the Brits just 85 to claim a victory.

One incident had occurred in the second innings which had left a very nasty taste in the mouths of the Australians and probably led to their reaction in the final English innings. That was when the novice Sam Jones played a ball which was picked up by an English fielder who tossed it back to the bowler. At that stage Jones left his crease to pat down some damage on the turf, a more or less routine operation. Dr Grace thought otherwise and seizing the ball promptly ran Jones out.

The Australian team members couldn't believe such unsporting action

PUNCH takes a tilt at the Disgraced Dr Grace

The Australians came down like a wolf on the fold

The Mary-Bone Cracks for a trifle were bowled.

Our Grace before dinner was very soon done

And our Grace after dinner did not get a run.

IN AFFECTIONATE REMEMBRANCE

OF

ENGLISH CRICKET

WHICH DIED AT THE OVAL

ON

29th *August* 1882,

Deeply lamented by a large circle of sorrowing
friends and acquaintances.

R. I. P.

N.B.—The body will be cremated, and the ashes
taken to Australia.

This is the Memoriam Notice Published by the London Sporting Times.

and neither could a lot of the English players judging by their attitudes. Dr Grace received a scathing condemnation in the English press for what they conceived to be an outrageously unfair act, particularly against a youngster playing his first major game. It was an incident that caused much damage to Grace's reputation. In the dressing room of Lords it was an action that met with outrage amongst the Australian players and when they took to the field for the final round of play they were out for revenge.

It was Spofforth who came to the rescue of the Australian team with an incredible spell of bowling. With four wickets down and only 32 runs needed to clinch the game England was still right on top. Then Spofforth bowled ten consecutive unplayable overs for only two runs. In that period Lytleton had stayed down the bowler's end. Spofforth believed he could bowl Lytleton out and he arranged with Murdoch for Bannerman to allow a ball to pass so that Lytleton would be facing up to Spofforth, who promptly bowled him out.

Then, in quick succession, Spofforth and Boyle bowled out the four remaining players to win the match by seven runs, to the utter astonishment of the very silenced crowd of spectators. Spofforth finished the match with seven wickets for 46 in the first innings and seven wickets for 44 in the second – a record that stood for many years.

The next week Punch magazine congratulated the Australians as follows:

Well done, Cornstalks. Whipt us
Fair and square.
Was it luck that tripped us?
Was it square?
Kangaroos' Land's "Demon", on his own
Want of "devil", coolness, nerve, backbone?

But it was the action of the London Sporting Times which made the most lasting impression of the match when the following day it published in traditional style a Memoriam Notice, "In affectionate Remembrance of English Cricket which died at The Oval on 29th August 1882, deeply lamented by a large circle of sorrowing friends and acquaintances R.I.P.

N.B. – the Body will be cremated, and the ashes taken to Australia."

Actually the latter action was not taken at the time and it was left to Trevor Bailey in his book The History of Cricket to explain what happened next:

"The following winter 1882-3 the Hon. Ivor Bligh took to Australia a team which won the rubber. At the end of the third match the stumps were burnt by some Australian ladies, who sealed up the ashes in an urn and presented them to the English Captain. He bequeathed them in his will to the MCC and they have remained at Lords ever since."

From time to time the Australians have suggested that after winning a test series in England they should be allowed to transport the actual ashes home Down Under, but the MCC has stoutly resisted such heretical ideas. Firstly they claimed that the urn was too fragile for transportation, and in more recent times they have ducked under the excuse that the ashes don't belong to them: that they only hold them on loan from the original trustees of the Honorable Ivor Bligh's Estate.

So it seems that the Ashes, which are fought over so strenuously from time to time, must remain in the firm grip of the MCC, no matter who is the winner of them.

Which seems to be an ideal note on which to conclude this brief history of the first eighty years of Australian Cricket.